VOLUME ONE

The WORD @ work

Scriptures for the Workplace

INCLUDING TOPICS ON
MONEY • CHARACTER • ETHICS • PEOPLE SKILLS

DR. J. VICTOR &
CATHERINE B. EAGAN

Workplace Wisdom® Publishing, L. L. C.
Orchard Lake, Michigan

Unless otherwise indicated, all Scripture quotations are taken from the Holy Bible, New International Version®. Copyright © 1973, 1978, 1984 by International Bible Society. Used by permission.

Scriptural quotations marked (AMP) are taken from The Amplified Bible. Old Testament copyright © 1965, 1987 by Zondervan Corporation, Grand Rapids, MI. New Testament copyright © 1958, 1987 by the Lockman Foundation, LaHabra, CA. Used by permission.

Scriptural quotations marked (KJV) are taken from The King James Version of the Bible.

The Word @ Work: Scriptures for the Workplace
Volume One

ISBN 0-9678889-4-8
Copyright © 2003 by
Workplace Wisdom Publishing, L. L. C.
Orchard Lake, Michigan

Contents

Dedication

The Word @ Work, Scriptures for the Workplace, Volume One is dedicated to every Christian who truly believes in the power of the Word of God and who heretofore went into the workplace unaided by its power.

Also to Jada Durham, our beloved niece, who went home to be with the Lord during our final preparation of this book.

Acknowledgements

We first want to acknowledge our Lord and Savior Jesus Christ and our Father God who gives us all things to enjoy. We are especially thankful for the joy of a loving and fulfilling relationship. We delight in the gift we call marriage. We deeply love each other and the work that God has called us to accomplish in the earth for His Kingdom to be established.

We are eternally grateful to our parents — both Mrs. Adele H. Cartey and Mrs. E. Louise Eagan who have not only been our faithful teachers but who have become our faithful students. Oh, what a joy! We are honored by God who chose them to steward us through this life.

To our Pastor, Bishop Keith A. Butler, Sr. and Minister Deborah L. Butler, we shall ever be eternally grateful to them for teaching us the power and importance of the Word of God. May we fulfill our purpose in such a manner that their report as the Shepherds for our souls is excellent.

We thank LaTanya Terry, Graphic Designer, Danyelle Buford, Administrative Assistant, Geralda Sellers, and Denise Stinson, Literary Agent.

Introduction

God wants to empower His people in the workplace with His Word. *The Word @ Work, Scriptures for the Workplace* is chock full of scriptures which will aid every believer in taking their rightful place at work.

The Word @Work, Scriptures for the Workplace, Volume One delineates scriptures in the areas of *Money, Godly Character, Godly Ethics, and Godly People Skills.* Christians face the same challenges as their non-Christian counterparts; however, we should excel, succeed, and overcome because we are empowered through the Word of God.

Too often The Body of Christ has gone into the workplace unaided with the Word of God. *The Word @ Work* is designed to systematically allow its readers to quickly go directly to scriptures on subjects near and dear to the heart regarding the workplace. It's through reading *The Word @ Work*, which is the Word of God, that readers will find peace, encouragement, strength, power, edification, exhortation, joy, centering, focus, and the ability to be Christ-like on the job.

Money is at the root of many business decisions and the Christian needs God's direction and leading to properly handle such matters and experience the prosperity that is so evidently an inheritance for every believer.

Godly Character development is the essence of the Christian walk. A daily dose of *The Word @ Work* will set every believer on the right path to operate with the mind of Christ.

Godly Ethics is a priceless commodity in today's business world. *The Word @ Work* stimulates its readers to serve God at all cost knowing that our Heavenly Father has called us to a life style of integrity in the workplace, for which we will be richly rewarded.

Godly People Skills are vital for success in the workplace. God loves people. The heart of God is for people and He wants us to treat people in a godly fashion. *The Word @ Work* dissects the Bible and provides easy access to jump-start your love walk at work.

Every Christian is encouraged and challenged to read the wisdom found in *The Word @ Work* and take the wisdom of God into the workplace.

Dr. J. Victor Eagan
Mrs. Catherine B. Eagan

Part One

Love of Money @ Work

Wealth and Riches @ Work

Love of Money @ Work

When you have eaten and are satisfied, praise the LORD your God for the good land he has given you. Be careful that you do not forget the LORD your God, failing to observe his commands, his laws and his decrees that I am giving you this day. Otherwise, when you eat and are satisfied, when you build fine houses and settle down, and when your herds and flocks grow large and your silver and gold increase and all you have is multiplied, then your heart will become proud and you will forget the LORD your God, who brought you out of Egypt, out of the land of slavery. You may say to yourself, "My power and the strength of my hands have produced this wealth for me." But remember the LORD your God, for it is he who gives you the ability to produce wealth, and so confirms his covenant, which he swore to your forefathers, as it is today.

Deuteronomy 8:10-14,17-18

Better the little that the righteous have than the wealth of many wicked;

Psalm 37:16

Man is a mere phantom as he goes to and fro: He bustles about, but only in vain; he heaps up wealth, not knowing who will get it.

Psalm 39:6

Those who trust in their wealth and boast of their great riches? No man

can redeem the lie of another or give to God a ransom for him — the
ransom for a life is costly, no payment is ever enough — that he should
live on forever and not see decay. For all can see that wise men die; the
foolish and the senseless alike perish and leave their wealth to others.

Psalm 49:6-10

Ill-gotten treasures are of no value, but righteousness delivers from
death.

Proverbs 10:2

Lazy hands make a man poor, but diligent hands bring wealth.

Proverbs 10:4

The wealth of the rich is their fortified city, but poverty is the ruin of
the poor.

Proverbs 10:15

The blessing of the LORD brings wealth, and he adds no trouble to it.

Proverbs 10:22

Wealth is worthless in the day of wrath, but righteousness delivers from
death.

Proverbs 11:4

Whoever trusts in his riches will fall, but the righteous will thrive like a
green leaf.

Proverbs 11:28

One man pretends to be rich, yet has nothing; another pretends to be
poor, yet has great wealth. A man's riches may ransom his life, but a
poor man hears no threat.

Proverbs 13:7-8

A good man leaves an inheritance for his children's children, but a sinner's
wealth is stored up for the righteous.

Proverbs 13:22

The wealth of the wise is their crown, but the folly of fools yields folly.

Proverbs 14:24

The house of the righteous contains great treasure, but the income of the wicked brings them trouble.

Proverbs 15:6

Better a little with the fear of the LORD than great wealth with turmoil. Better a meal of vegetables where there is love than a fattened calf with hatred.

Proverbs 15:16-17

Better a little with righteousness than much gain with injustice.

Proverbs 16:8

The wealth of the rich is their fortified city; they imagine it an unscalable wall.

Proverbs 18:11

Wealth brings many friends, but a poor man's friend deserts him.

Proverbs 19:4

Houses and wealth are inherited from parents, but a prudent wife is from the LORD.

Proverbs 19:14

A fortune made by a lying tongue is a fleeting vapor and a deadly snare.

Proverbs 21:6

He who pursues righteousness and love finds life, prosperity and honor.

Proverbs 21:21

Humility and the fear of the LORD bring wealth and honor and life.

Proverbs 22:4

Do not wear yourself out to get rich; have the wisdom to show restraint. Cast but a glance at riches, and they are gone, for they will surely sprout wings and fly off to the sky like an eagle.

Proverbs 23:4-5

Be sure you know the condition of your flocks, give careful attention to your herds; for riches do not endure forever, and a crown is not secure for all generations.

Proverbs 27:23-24

He who increases his wealth by exorbitant interest amasses it for another, who will be kind to the poor.

Proverbs 28:8

A faithful man will be richly blessed, but one eager to get rich will not go unpunished.

Proverbs 28:20

A stingy man is eager to get rich and is unaware that poverty awaits him.

Proverbs 28:22

Keep falsehood and lies far from me; give me neither poverty nor riches, but give me only my daily bread. Otherwise, I may have too much and disown you and say, 'Who is the LORD?' Or I may become poor and steal, and so dishonor the name of my God.

Proverbs 30:8-9

The increase from the land is taken by all; the king himself profits from the fields. Whoever loves money never has money enough; whoever loves wealth is never satisfied with his income. This too is meaningless. As goods increase, so do those who consume them. And what benefit are they to the owner except to feast his eyes on them? The sleep of a laborer is sweet, whether he eats little or much, but the abundance of a rich man permits him no sleep. I have seen a grievous evil under the sun: wealth hoarded to the harm of its owner, or wealth lost through some misfortune, so that when he has a son there is nothing left for him. Naked a man comes from his mother's womb, and as he comes, so he departs. He takes nothing from his labor that he can carry in his hand. This too is a grievous evil: As a man comes, so he departs, and what does he gain, since he toils for the wind? All his days he eats in darkness, with great frustration, affliction and anger.

Then I realized that it is good and proper for a man to eat and drink, and to find satisfaction in his toilsome labor under the sun during the few days of life God has given him — for this is his lot. Moreover, when God gives any man wealth and possessions, and enables him to enjoy them, to accept his lot and be happy in his work — this is a gift of God. He seldom reflects on the days of his life, because God keeps him occupied with gladness of heart.

Ecclesiastes 5:9-20

Wisdom, like an inheritance, is a good thing and benefits those who see the sun. Wisdom is a shelter as money is a shelter, but the advantage of knowledge is this: that wisdom preserves the life of its possessor.

Ecclesiastes 7:11-12

Do not store up for yourselves treasures on earth, where moth and rust destroy, and where thieves break in and steal. But store up for yourselves treasures in heaven, where moth and rust do not destroy, and where thieves do not break in and steal. For where your treasure is, there your heart will be also.

Matthew 6:19-21

But seek first his kingdom and his righteousness, and all these things will be given to you as well.

Matthew 6:33

The one who received the seed that fell among the thorns is the man who hears the word, but the worries of this life and the deceitfulness of wealth choke it, making it unfruitful.

Matthew 13:22

Now a man came up to Jesus and asked, "Teacher, what good thing must I do to get eternal life?" "Why do you ask me about what is good?" Jesus replied. "There is only One who is good. If you want to enter life, obey the commandments." "Which ones?" The man inquired. Jesus replied, "'Do not murder, do not commit adultery, do not steal, do not give false testimony, honor your father and mother,' and 'love your neighbor as yourself.'" "All these I have kept," the young man said. "What do I still lack?" Jesus answered, "If you want to be perfect, go, sell your possessions and give to the poor, and you will have treasure in heaven. Then come, follow me." When the young man heard this, he went away sad, because he had great wealth. Then Jesus said to his disciples, "I tell you the truth, it is hard for a rich man to enter the kingdom of heaven. Again I tell you, it is easier for a camel to go through the eye of a needle than for a rich man to enter the kingdom of God." When the disciples heard this, they were greatly astonished and asked, "Who then can be saved?" Jesus looked at them and said, "With man this is impossible, but with God all things are possible." Peter answered him, "We have left everything to follow you! What then will there be for us?" Jesus said to them, "I tell you the truth, at the renewal of all things, when the Son of Man sits on his glorious throne, you who have followed me will also sit on twelve thrones, judging the twelve tribes of Israel. And everyone who has left houses or brothers or sisters or father or mother or children or fields for my sake will receive a hundred times as much and will inherit eternal life."

Matthew 19:16-29

But the worries of this life, the deceitfulness of wealth and the desires for other things come in and choke the word, making it unfruitful.

Mark 4:19

Then he said to them, "Watch out! Be on your guard against all kinds of greed; a man's life does not consist in the abundance of his possessions."

Luke 12:15

But godliness with contentment is great gain. For we brought nothing into the world, and we can take nothing out of it. But if we have food and clothing, we will be content with that. People who want to get rich fall into temptation and a trap and into many foolish and harmful desires that plunge men into ruin and destruction. For the love of money is a root of all kinds of evil. Some people, eager for money, have wandered from the faith and pierced themselves with many griefs. But you, man of God, flee from all this, and pursue righteousness, godliness, faith, love, endurance and gentleness.

1 Timothy 6:6-11

Command those who are rich in this present world not to be arrogant nor to put their hope in wealth, which is so uncertain, but to put their hope in God, who richly provides us with everything for our enjoyment. Command them to do good, to be rich in good deeds, and to be generous and willing to share. In this way they will lay up treasure for themselves as a firm foundation for the coming age, so that they may take hold of the life that is truly life.

1 Timothy 6:17-19

If anyone has material possessions and sees his brother in need but has no pity on him, how can the love of God be in him?

1 John 3:17

Financial Increase @ Work

Love of Money @ Work

Isaac planted crops in that land and the same year reaped a hundred-fold, because the LORD blessed him.

Genesis 26:12

But remember the LORD your God, for it is he who gives you the ability to produce wealth, and so confirms his covenant, which he swore to your forefathers, as it is today.

Deuteronomy 8:18

If you fully obey the LORD your God and carefully follow all his commands I give you today, the LORD your God will set you high above all the nations on earth. All these blessings will come upon you and accompany you if you obey the LORD your God: You will be blessed in the city and blessed in the country. The fruit of your womb will be blessed, and the crops of your land and the young of your livestock — the calves of your herds and the lambs of your flocks. Your basket and your kneading trough will be blessed. You will be blessed when you come in and blessed when you go out. The LORD will grant that the enemies who rise up against you will be defeated before you. They will come at you from one direction but flee from you in seven. The LORD will send a blessing on your barns and on everything you put your hand to. The LORD your God will bless you in the land he is giving you. The LORD will establish you

as his holy people, as he promised you on oath, if you keep the commands of the LORD your God and walk in his ways. Then all the peoples
on earth will see that you are called by the name of the LORD, and they
will fear you. The LORD will grant you abundant prosperity — in the
fruit of your womb, the young of your livestock and the crops of your
ground — in the land he swore to your forefathers to give you. The
LORD will open the heavens, the storehouse of his bounty, to send rain
on your land in season and to bless all the work of your hands. You will
lend to many nations but will borrow from none. The LORD will make you
the head, not the tail. If you pay attention to the commands of the
LORD your God that I give you this day and carefully follow them, you
will always be at the top, never at the bottom. Do not turn aside from
any of the commands I give you today, to the right or to the left,
following other gods and serving them.

Deuteronomy 28:1-4

Submit to God and be at peace with him; in this way prosperity will
come to you.

Job 22:21

Who, then, is the man that fears the LORD? He will instruct him in the
way chosen for him. He will spend his days in prosperity, and his descendants will inherit the land.

Psalm 25:12-13

Blessed are all who fear the LORD, who walk in his ways. You will eat the
fruit of your labor; blessings and prosperity will be yours.

Psalm 128:1-2

My son, do not forget my teaching, but keep my commands in your
heart, for they will prolong your life many years and bring you prosperity.

Proverbs 3:1-2

Honor the LORD with your wealth, with the firstfruits of all your crops;
then your barns will be filled to overflowing, and your vats will brim
over with new wine.

Proverbs 3:9-10

She is a tree of life to those who embrace her; those who lay hold of her will be blessed.

Proverbs 3:18

The LORD's curse is on the house of the wicked, but he blesses the home of the righteous.

Proverbs 3:33

Lazy hands make a man poor, but diligent hands bring wealth.

Proverbs 10:4

He who gathers crops in summer is a wise son, but he who sleeps during harvest is a disgraceful son.

Proverbs 10:5

Blessings crown the head of the righteous, but violence overwhelms the mouth of the wicked.

Proverbs 10:6

The wise in heart accept commands, but a chattering fool comes to ruin.

Proverbs 10:8

The man of integrity walks securely, but he who takes crooked paths will be found out.

Proverbs 10:9

The wages of the righteous bring them life, but the income of the wicked brings them punishment.

Proverbs 10:16

The blessing of the LORD brings wealth, and he adds no trouble to it.

Proverbs 10:22

The wicked man earns deceptive wages, but he who sows righteousness reaps a sure reward.

Proverbs 11:18

For lack of guidance a nation falls, but many advisers make victory sure.

Proverbs 11:14

The desire of the righteous ends only in good, but the hope of the wicked only in wrath.

Proverbs 11:23

One man gives freely, yet gains even more; another withholds unduly, but comes to poverty.

Proverbs 11:24

A generous man will prosper; he who refreshes others will himself be refreshed.

Proverbs 11:25

People curse the man who hoards grain, but blessing crowns him who is willing to sell.

Proverbs 11:26

He who works his land will have abundant food, but he who chases fantasies lacks judgment.

Proverbs 12:11

From the fruit of his lips a man is filled with good things as surely as the work of his hands rewards him.

Proverbs 12:14

The sluggard craves and gets nothing, but the desires of the diligent are fully satisfied.

Proverbs 13:4

Dishonest money dwindles away, but he who gathers money little by little makes it grow.

Proverbs 13:11

He who scorns instruction will pay for it, but he who respects a command is rewarded.

Proverbs 13:13

Misfortune pursues the sinner, but prosperity is the reward of the righteous. A good man leaves an inheritance for his children's children, but a sinner's wealth is stored up for the righteous.

Proverbs 13:21-22

Where there are no oxen, the manger is empty, but from the strength of an ox comes an abundant harvest.

Proverbs 14:4

The house of the wicked will be destroyed, but the tent of the upright will flourish.

Proverbs 14:11

He who despises his neighbor sins, but blessed is he who is kind to the needy.

Proverbs 14:21

All hard work brings a profit, but mere talk leads only to poverty.

Proverbs 14:23

The house of the righteous contains great treasure, but the income of the wicked brings them trouble.

Proverbs 15:6

The way of the sluggard is blocked with thorns, but the path of the upright is a highway.

Proverbs 15:19

The tongue has the power of life and death, and those who love it will eat its fruit.

Proverbs 18:21

He who gets wisdom loves his own soul; he who cherishes understanding prospers.

Proverbs 19:8

He who is kind to the poor lends to the LORD, and he will reward him for what he has done.

Proverbs 19:17

The plans of the diligent lead to profit as surely as haste leads to poverty.

Proverbs 21:5

He who pursues righteousness and love finds life, prosperity and honor.

Proverbs 21:21

Humility and the fear of the LORD bring wealth and honor and life.

Proverbs 22:4

A generous man will himself be blessed, for he shares his food with the poor.

Proverbs 22:9

Do you see a man skilled in his work? He will serve before kings; he will not serve before obscure men.

Proverbs 22:29

By wisdom a house is built, and through understanding it is established; through knowledge its rooms are filled with rare and beautiful treasures.

Proverbs 24:3-4

He who leads the upright along an evil path will fall into his own trap, but the blameless will receive a good inheritance.

Proverbs 28:10

He who works his land will have abundant food, but the one who chases fantasies will have his fill of poverty.

Proverbs 28:19

A greedy man stirs up dissension, but he who trusts in the LORD will prosper.

Proverbs 28:25

To the man who pleases him, God gives wisdom, knowledge and happiness, but to the sinner he gives the task of gathering and storing up wealth to hand it over to the one who pleases God. This too is meaningless, a chasing after the wind.

Ecclesiastes 2:26

He who walks righteously and speaks what is right, who rejects gain from extortion and keeps his hand from accepting bribes, who stops his ears against plots of murder and shuts his eyes against contemplating evil — this is the man who will dwell on the heights, whose refuge will be the mountain fortress. His bread will be supplied, and water will not fail him.

Isaiah 33:15-16

Thus says the LORD, your Redeemer, the Holy One of Israel: "I am the LORD your God, who teaches you to profit, who leads you by the way you should go."

Isaiah 48:17 (NKJ)

Financial Ruin @ Work

Love of Money @ Work

However, if you do not obey the LORD your God and do not carefully follow all his commands and decrees I am giving you today, all these curses will come upon you and overtake you: You will be cursed in the city and cursed in the country. Your basket and your kneading trough will be cursed. The fruit of your womb will be cursed, and the crops of your land, and the calves of your herds and the lambs of your flocks. You will be cursed when you come in and cursed when you go out.

Deuteronomy 28:15-19

The LORD's curse is on the house of the wicked, but he blesses the home of the righteous.

Proverbs 3:33

My son, pay attention to my wisdom, listen well to my words of insight, that you may maintain discretion and your lips may preserve knowledge. For the lips of an adulteress drip honey, and her speech is smoother than oil; but in the end she is bitter as gall, sharp as a double-edged sword. Her feet go down to death; her steps lead straight to the grave. She gives no thought to the way of life; her paths are crooked, but she knows it not. Now then, my sons, listen to me; do not turn aside from what I say. Keep to a path far from her, do not go near the door of her house, lest you give your best strength to others and your years to one

19

who is cruel, lest strangers feast on your wealth and your toil enrich another man's house.

Proverbs 5:1-10

A scoundrel and villain, who goes about with a corrupt mouth, who winks with his eye, signals with his feet and motions with his fingers, who plots evil with deceit in his heart — he always stirs up dissension. Therefore disaster will overtake him in an instant; he will suddenly be destroyed — without remedy.

Proverbs 6:12-15

There are six things the LORD hates, seven that are detestable to him: haughty eyes, a lying tongue, hands that shed innocent blood, a heart that devises wicked schemes, feet that are quick to rush into evil, a false witness who pours out lies and a man who stirs up dissension among brothers.

Proverbs 6:16-19

But a man who commits adultery lacks judgment; whoever does so destroys himself.

Proverbs 6:32

The wise in heart accept commands, but a chattering fool comes to ruin.

Proverbs 10:8

He who winks maliciously causes grief, and a chattering fool comes to ruin.

Proverbs 10:10

Wise men store up knowledge, but the mouth of a fool invites ruin.

Proverbs 10:14

He who heeds discipline shows the way to life, but whoever ignores correction leads others astray.

Proverbs 10:17

The lips of the righteous nourish many, but fools die for lack of judgment.

Proverbs 10:21

When the storm has swept by, the wicked are gone, but the righteous stand firm forever.

Proverbs 10:25

The fear of the LORD adds length to life, but the years of the wicked are cut short.

Proverbs 10:27

The way of the LORD is a refuge for the righteous, but it is the ruin of those who do evil.

Proverbs 10:29

The integrity of the upright guides them, but the unfaithful are destroyed by their duplicity.

Proverbs 11:3

The righteousness of the blameless makes a straight way for them, but the wicked are brought down by their own wickedness.

Proverbs 11:5

He who puts up security for another will surely suffer, but whoever refuses to strike hands in pledge is safe.

Proverbs 11:15

The truly righteous man attains life, but he who pursues evil goes to his death.

Proverbs 11:19

The desire of the righteous ends only in good, but the hope of the wicked only in wrath.

Proverbs 11:23

One man gives freely, yet gains even more; another withholds unduly, but comes to poverty.

Proverbs 11:24

Whoever trusts in his riches will fall, but the righteous will thrive like a green leaf.

Proverbs 11:28

Whoever loves discipline loves knowledge, but he who hates correction is stupid.

Proverbs 12:1

Wicked men are overthrown and are no more, but the house of the righteous stands firm.

Proverbs 12:7

He who works his land will have abundant food, but he who chases fantasies lacks judgment.

Proverbs 12:11

He who guards his lips guards his life, but he who speaks rashly will come to ruin.

Proverbs 13:3

Dishonest money dwindles away, but he who gathers money little by little makes it grow.

Proverbs 13:11

He who ignores discipline comes to poverty and shame, but whoever heeds correction is honored.

Proverbs 13:18

He who walks with the wise grows wise, but a companion of fools suffers harm. Misfortune pursues the sinner, but prosperity is the reward of the righteous. A good man leaves an inheritance for his children's children, but a sinner's wealth is stored up for the righteous.

Proverbs 13:20-22

The house of the wicked will be destroyed, but the tent of the upright will flourish.

Proverbs 14:11

All hard work brings a profit, but mere talk leads only to poverty.

Proverbs 14:23

The house of the righteous contains great treasure, but the income of the wicked brings them trouble.

Proverbs 15:6

Pride goes before destruction, a haughty spirit before a fall.

Proverbs 16:18

A man of perverse heart does not prosper; he whose tongue is deceitful falls into trouble.

Proverbs 17:20

A fool's lips bring him strife, and his mouth invites a beating.

Proverbs 18:6

A fool's mouth is his undoing, and his lips are a snare to his soul.

Proverbs 18:7

The words of a gossip are like choice morsels; they go down to a man's inmost parts.

Proverbs 18:8

One who is slack in his work is brother to one who destroys.

Proverbs 18:9

The tongue has the power of life and death, and those who love it will eat its fruit.

Proverbs 18:21

A man of many companions may come to ruin, but there is a friend who sticks closer than a brother.

Proverbs 18:24

It is not good to have zeal without knowledge, nor to be hasty and miss the way.

Proverbs 19:2

A man's own folly ruins his life, yet his heart rages against the LORD.

Proverbs 19:3

Do not love sleep or you will grow poor; stay awake and you will have food to spare.

Proverbs 20:13

An inheritance quickly gained at the beginning will not be blessed at the end.

Proverbs 20:21

The plans of the diligent lead to profit as surely as haste leads to poverty.

Proverbs 21:5

The Righteous One takes note of the house of the wicked and brings the wicked to ruin.

Proverbs 21:12

A man who strays from the path of understanding comes to rest in the company of the dead.

Proverbs 21:16

He who loves pleasure will become poor; whoever loves wine and oil will never be rich.

Proverbs 21:17

The sluggard's craving will be the death of him, because his hands refuse to work.

Proverbs 21:25

He who sows wickedness reaps trouble, and the rod of his fury will be destroyed.

Proverbs 22:8

The mouth of an adulteress is a deep pit; he who is under the LORD's wrath will fall into it.

Proverbs 22:14

He who oppresses the poor to increase his wealth and he who gives gifts to the rich — both come to poverty.

Proverbs 22:16

Do not exploit the poor because they are poor and do not crush the needy in court, for the LORD will take up their case and will plunder those who plunder them.

Proverbs 22:22-23

Do not join those who drink too much wine or gorge themselves on meat, for drunkards and gluttons become poor, and drowsiness clothes them in rags.

Proverbs 23:20-21

For though a righteous man falls seven times, he rises again, but the wicked are brought down by calamity.

Proverbs 24:16

I went past the field of the sluggard, past the vineyard of the man who lacks judgment; thorns had come up everywhere, the ground was covered with weeds, and the stone wall was in ruins. I applied my heart to what I observed and learned a lesson from what I saw: A little sleep, a little slumber, a little folding of the hands to rest — and poverty will come on you like a bandit and scarcity like an armed man.

Proverbs 24:30-34

He who leads the upright along an evil path will fall into his own trap, but the blameless will receive a good inheritance.

Proverbs 28:10

He who conceals his sins does not prosper, but whoever confesses and renounces them finds mercy. Blessed is the man who always fears the LORD, but he who hardens his heart falls into trouble.

Proverbs 28:13-14

He whose walk is blameless is kept safe, but he whose ways are perverse will suddenly fall. He who works his land will have abundant food, but the one who chases fantasies will have his fill of poverty.

Proverbs 28:18-19

A stingy man is eager to get rich and is unaware that poverty awaits him.

Proverbs 28:22

A man who remains stiff-necked after many rebukes will suddenly be destroyed — without remedy.

Proverbs 29:1

A man who loves wisdom brings joy to his father, but a companion of prostitutes squanders his wealth.

Proverbs 29:3

Do not spend your strength on women, your vigor on those who ruin kings.

Proverbs 31:3

And he said to me, "This is the curse that is going out over the whole land; for according to what it says on one side, every thief will be banished, and according to what it says on the other, everyone who swears falsely will be banished."

Zechariah 5:3

People who want to get rich fall into temptation and a trap and into many foolish and harmful desires that plunge men into ruin and destruction. For the love of money is a root of all kinds of evil. Some people, eager for money, have wandered from the faith and pierced themselves with many griefs.

1 Timothy 6:9-10

Getting Rich Quickly @ Work

Love of Money @ Work

Be still before the LORD and wait patiently for him; do not fret when men succeed in their ways, when they carry out their wicked schemes.

Psalm 37:7

Teach me, O LORD, to follow your decrees; then I will keep them to the end. Give me understanding, and I will keep your law and obey it with all my heart. Direct me in the path of your commands, for there I find delight. Turn my heart toward your statutes and not toward selfish gain. Turn my eyes away from worthless things; preserve my life according to your word.

Psalm 119:33-37

Trust in the LORD with all your heart and lean not on your own understanding; in all your ways acknowledge him, and he will make your paths straight.

Proverbs 3:5-6

The blessing of the LORD brings wealth, and he adds no trouble to it.

Proverbs 10:22

He who works his land will have abundant food, but he who chases fantasies lacks judgment.

Proverbs 12:11

27

Dishonest money dwindles away, but he who gathers money little by little makes it grow.

Proverbs 13:11

He who walks with the wise grows wise, but a companion of fools suffers harm. Misfortune pursues the sinner, but prosperity is the reward of the righteous.

Proverbs 13:20-21

There is a way that seems right to a man, but in the end it leads to death.

Proverbs 14:12

All hard work brings a profit, but mere talk leads only to poverty.

Proverbs 14:23

A greedy man brings trouble to his family, but he who hates bribes will live.

Proverbs 15:27

It is not good to have zeal without knowledge, nor to be hasty and miss the way.

Proverbs 19:2

An inheritance quickly gained at the beginning will not be blessed at the end.

Proverbs 20:21

The plans of the diligent lead to profit as surely as haste leads to poverty.

Proverbs 21:5

Do not wear yourself out to get rich; have the wisdom to show restraint. Cast but a glance at riches, and they are gone, for they will surely sprout wings and fly off to the sky like an eagle.

Proverbs 23:4-5

He who works his land will have abundant food, but the one who chases fantasies will have his fill of poverty. A faithful man will be richly blessed, but one eager to get rich will not go unpunished.

Proverbs 28:19-20

To show partiality is not good — yet a man will do wrong for a piece of bread. A stingy man is eager to get rich and is unaware that poverty awaits him.

Proverbs 28:21-22

Like a partridge that hatches eggs it did not lay is the man who gains riches by unjust means. When his life is half gone, they will desert him, and in the end he will prove to be a fool.

Jeremiah 17:11

People who want to get rich fall into temptation and a trap and into many foolish and harmful desires that plunge men into ruin and destruction. For the love of money is a root of all kinds of evil. Some people, eager for money, have wandered from the faith and pierced themselves with many griefs. But you, man of God, flee from all this, and pursue righteousness, godliness, faith, love, endurance and gentleness.

1 Timothy 6:9-11

Greed @ Work

Love of Money @ Work

You shall not covet your neighbor's house. You shall not covet your neighbor's wife, or his manservant or maidservant, his ox or donkey, or anything that belongs to your neighbor.

Exodus 20:17

Teach me, O LORD, to follow your decrees; then I will keep them to the end. Give me understanding, and I will keep your law and obey it with all my heart. Direct me in the path of your commands, for there I find delight. Turn my heart toward your statutes and not toward selfish gain.

Psalm 119:33-36

One man gives freely, yet gains even more; another withholds unduly, but comes to poverty. A generous man will prosper; he who refreshes others will himself be refreshed. People curse the man who hoards grain, but blessing crowns him who is willing to sell.

Proverbs 11:24-26

Whoever trusts in his riches will fall, but the righteous will thrive like a green leaf.

Proverbs 11:28

The wicked desire the plunder of evil men, but the root of the righteous flourishes.

Proverbs 12:12

A greedy man brings trouble to his family, but he who hates bribes will live.

Proverbs 15:27

An unfriendly man pursues selfish ends; he defies all sound judgment.

Proverbs 18:1

In the house of the wise are stores of choice food and oil, but a foolish man devours all he has.

Proverbs 21:20

Do not wear yourself out to get rich; have the wisdom to show restraint. Cast but a glance at riches, and they are gone, for they will surely sprout wings and fly off to the sky like an eagle.

Proverbs 23:4-5

Death and Destruction are never satisfied, and neither are the eyes of man.

Proverbs 27:20

A greedy man stirs up dissension, but he who trusts in the LORD will prosper.

Proverbs 28:25

Two things I ask of you, O LORD; do not refuse me before I die: Keep falsehood and lies far from me; give me neither poverty nor riches, but give me only my daily bread. Otherwise, I may have too much and disown you and say, Who is the LORD? Or I may become poor and steal, and so dishonor the name of my God.

Proverbs 30:7-9

And I saw that all labor and all achievement spring from man's envy of his neighbor. This too is meaningless, a chasing after the wind.

Ecclesiastes 4:4

Again I saw something meaningless under the sun: There was a man all alone; he had neither son nor brother. There was no end to his toil, yet his eyes were not content with his wealth. "For whom am I toiling," he asked, "and why am I depriving myself of enjoyment?" This too is meaningless — a miserable business!

Ecclesiastes 4:7-8

Whoever loves money never has money enough; whoever loves wealth is never satisfied with his income. This too is meaningless. As goods increase, so do those who consume them. And what benefit are they to the owner except to feast his eyes on them?

Ecclesiastes 5:10-11

I have seen a grievous evil under the sun: wealth hoarded to the harm of its owner, or wealth lost through some misfortune, so that when he has a son there is nothing left for him. Naked a man comes from his mother's womb, and as he comes, so he departs. He takes nothing from his labor that he can carry in his hand. This too is a grievous evil: As a man comes, so he departs, and what does he gain, since he toils for the wind? All his days he eats in darkness, with great frustration, affliction and anger. Then I realized that it is good and proper for a man to eat and drink, and to find satisfaction in his toilsome labor under the sun during the few days of life God has given him — for this is his lot. Moreover, when God gives any man wealth and possessions, and enables him to enjoy them, to accept his lot and be happy in his work — this is a gift of God. He seldom reflects on the days of his life, because God keeps him occupied with gladness of heart.

Ecclesiastes 5:13-20

All man's efforts are for his mouth, yet his appetite is never satisfied.

Ecclesiastes 6:7

I the LORD search the heart and examine the mind, to reward a man according to his conduct, according to what his deeds deserve. Like a partridge that hatches eggs it did not lay is the man who gains riches by unjust means. When his life is half gone, they will desert him, and in the end he will prove to be a fool.

Jeremiah 17:10-11

Woe to those who plan iniquity, to those who plot evil on their beds! At morning's light they carry it out because it is in their power to do it.

They covet fields and seize them, and houses, and take them. They defraud a man of his home, a fellowman of his inheritance. Therefore, the LORD says: "I am planning disaster against this people, from which you cannot save yourselves. You will no longer walk proudly, for it will be a time of calamity."

Micah 2:1-3

Do not store up for yourselves treasures on earth, where moth and rust destroy, and where thieves break in and steal. But store up for yourselves treasures in heaven, where moth and rust do not destroy, and where thieves do not break in and steal. For where your treasure is, there your heart will be also.

Matthew 6:19-21

No one can serve two masters. Either he will hate the one and love the other, or he will be devoted to the one and despise the other. You cannot serve both God and Money.

Matthew 6:24

So do not worry, saying, 'What shall we eat?' or 'What shall we drink?' or 'What shall we wear?' For the pagans run after all these things, and your heavenly Father knows that you need them. But seek first his kingdom and his righteousness, and all these things will be given to you as well.

Matthew 6:31-33

What good will it be for a man if he gains the whole world, yet forfeits his soul? Or what can a man give in exchange for his soul?

Matthew 16:26

Then Jesus said to his disciples, "I tell you the truth, it is hard for a rich man to enter the kingdom of heaven. Again I tell you, it is easier for a camel to go through the eye of a needle than for a rich man to enter the kingdom of God." When the disciples heard this, they were greatly astonished and asked, "Who then can be saved?" Jesus looked at them and said, "With man this is impossible, but with God all things are possible."

Matthew 19:23-26

He went on: "What comes out of a man is what makes him 'unclean.' For from within, out of men's hearts, come evil thoughts, sexual immorality, theft, murder, adultery, greed, malice, deceit, lewdness, envy, slander, arrogance and folly. All these evils come from inside and make a man 'unclean.'"

Mark 7:20-23

Then he said to them, "Watch out! Be on your guard against all kinds of greed; a man's life does not consist in the abundance of his possessions." And he told them this parable: "The ground of a certain rich man produced a good crop. He thought to himself, 'What shall I do? I have no place to store my crops.' "Then he said, 'This is what I'll do. I will tear down my barns and build bigger ones, and there I will store all my grain and my goods. And I'll say to myself, "You have plenty of good things laid up for many years. Take life easy; eat, drink and be merry."' "But God said to him, 'You fool! This very night your life will be demanded from you. Then who will get what you have prepared for yourself?' "This is how it will be with anyone who stores up things for himself but is not rich toward God."

Luke 12:15-21

Jesus looked at him and said, "How hard it is for the rich to enter the kingdom of God! Indeed, it is easier for a camel to go through the eye of a needle than for a rich man to enter the kingdom of God." Those who heard this asked, "Who then can be saved?" Jesus replied, "What is impossible with men is possible with God." Peter said to him, "We have left all we had to follow you! "I tell you the truth," Jesus said to them, "no one who has left home or wife or brothers or parents or children for the sake of the kingdom of God will fail to receive many times as much in this age and, in the age to come, eternal life."

Luke 18:24-30

The commandments, "Do not commit adultery," "Do not murder," "Do not steal," "Do not covet," and whatever other commandment there may be, are summed up in this one rule: "Love your neighbor as yourself." Love does no harm to its neighbor. Therefore, love is the fulfillment of the law.

Romans 13:9-10

Do you not know that the wicked will not inherit the kingdom of God? Do not be deceived: Neither the sexually immoral nor idolaters nor adulterers nor male prostitutes nor homosexual offenders nor thieves nor the greedy nor drunkards nor slanderers nor swindlers will inherit the kingdom of God. And that is what some of you were. But you were washed, you were sanctified, you were justified in the name of the Lord Jesus Christ and by the Spirit of our God.

1 Corinthians 6:9-11

But among you there must not be even a hint of sexual immorality, or of any kind of impurity, or of greed, because these are improper for God's holy people. Nor should there be obscenity, foolish talk or coarse joking, which are out of place, but rather thanksgiving. For of this you can be sure: No immoral, impure or greedy person — such a man is an idolater — has any inheritance in the kingdom of Christ and of God. Let no one deceive you with empty words, for because of such things God's wrath comes on those who are disobedient. Therefore, do not be partners with them.

Ephesians 5:3-7

Put to death, therefore, whatever belongs to your earthly nature: sexual immorality, impurity, lust, evil desires and greed, which is idolatry. Because of these, the wrath of God is coming. You used to walk in these ways, in the life you once lived.

Colossians 3:5-7

Men of corrupt mind, who have been robbed of the truth and who think that godliness is a means to financial gain. But godliness with contentment is great gain. For we brought nothing into the world, and we can take nothing out of it. But if we have food and clothing, we will be content with that. People who want to get rich fall into temptation and a trap and into many foolish and harmful desires that plunge men into ruin and destruction. For the love of money is a root of all kinds of evil. Some people, eager for money, have wandered from the faith and pierced themselves with many griefs. But you, man of God, flee from all this, and pursue righteousness, godliness, faith, love, endurance and gentleness.

1 Timothy 6:6-11

Command those who are rich in this present world not to be arrogant nor to put their hope in wealth, which is so uncertain, but to put their hope in God, who richly provides us with everything for our enjoyment. Command them to do good, to be rich in good deeds, and to be generous and willing to share. In this way they will lay up treasure for themselves as a firm foundation for the coming age, so that they may take hold of the life that is truly life.

1 Timothy 6:17-19

But mark this: There will be terrible times in the last days. People will be lovers of themselves, lovers of money, boastful, proud, abusive, disobedient to their parents, ungrateful, unholy, without love, unforgiving, slanderous, without self-control, brutal, not lovers of the good, treacherous, rash, conceited, lovers of pleasure rather than lovers of God — having a form of godliness but denying its power. Have nothing to do with them.

2 Timothy 3:1-5

Keep your lives free from the love of money and be content with what you have, because God has said, "Never will I leave you; never will I forsake you."

Hebrews 13:5

What causes fights and quarrels among you? Don't they come from your desires that battle within you? You want something but don't get it. You kill and covet, but you cannot have what you want. You quarrel and fight. You do not have, because you do not ask God. When you ask, you do not receive, because you ask with wrong motives, that you may spend what you get on your pleasures. You adulterous people, don't you know that friendship with the world is hatred toward God? Anyone who chooses to be a friend of the world becomes an enemy of God.

James 4:1-4

Do not love the world or anything in the world. If anyone loves the world, the love of the Father is not in him. For everything in the world — the cravings of sinful man, the lust of his eyes and the boasting of what he has and does — comes not from the Father but from the world.

The world and its desires pass away, but the man who does the will of God lives forever.

1 John 2:15-17

The Love of
Money @ Work

Love of Money @ Work

"You shall have no other gods before me. You shall not make for yourself an idol in the form of anything in heaven above or on the earth beneath or in the waters below." "You shall not bow down to them or worship them; for I, the LORD your God, am a jealous God, punishing the children for the sin of the fathers to the third and fourth generation of those who hate me, but showing love to a thousand of those who love me and keep my commandments."

Exodus 20:3-6

"You shall not covet your neighbor's house. You shall not covet your neighbor's wife, or his manservant or maidservant, his ox or donkey, or anything that belongs to your neighbor."

Exodus 20:17

Fear the LORD your God, serve him only and take your oaths in his name. Do not follow other gods, the gods of the peoples around you.

Deuteronomy 6:13-14

You may say to yourself, "My power and the strength of my hands have produced this wealth for me." But remember the LORD your God, for it is he who gives you the ability to produce wealth, and so confirms his covenant, which he swore to your forefathers, as it is today. If you ever forget the LORD your God and follow other gods and worship and bow down to them, I testify against you today that you will surely be destroyed.

Deuteronomy 8:17-19

"If I have put my trust in gold or said to pure gold, 'You are my security,' if I have rejoiced over my great wealth, the fortune my hands had gained, if I have regarded the sun in its radiance or the moon moving in splendor, so that my heart was secretly enticed and my hand offered them a kiss of homage, then these also would be sins to be judged, for I would have been unfaithful to God on high.

Job 31:24-28

Those who trust in their wealth and boast of their great riches? No man can redeem the life of another or give to God a ransom for him — the ransom for a life is costly, no payment is ever enough.

Psalm 49:6-8

Surely God will bring you down to everlasting ruin: He will snatch you up and tear you from your tent; he will uproot you from the land of the living. Selah. The righteous will see and fear; they will laugh at him, saying, here now is the man who did not make God his stronghold but trusted in his great wealth and grew strong by destroying others! But I am like an olive tree flourishing in the house of God; I trust in God's unfailing love for ever and ever. I will praise you forever for what you have done; in your name I will hope, for your name is good. I will praise you in the presence of your saints.

Psalm 52:5-9

Do not trust in extortion or take pride in stolen goods; though your riches increase, do not set your heart on them.

Psalm 62:10

Such is the end of all who go after ill-gotten gain; it takes away the lives of those who get it.

Proverbs 1:19

The wealth of the rich is their fortified city, but poverty is the ruin of the poor.

Proverbs 10:15

Whoever trusts in his riches will fall, but the righteous will thrive like a green leaf.

Proverbs 11:28

There was a man all alone; he had neither son nor brother. There was no end to his toil, yet his eyes were not content with his wealth. "For whom am I toiling," he asked, "and why am I depriving myself of enjoyment?" This too is meaningless — a miserable business!

Ecclessiastes 4:8

Whoever loves money never has money enough; whoever loves wealth is never satisfied with his income. This too is meaningless. As goods increase, so do those who consume them. And what benefit are they to the owner except to feast his eyes on them?

Ecclessiastes 5:10-11

In you men accept bribes to shed blood; you take usury and excessive interest and make unjust gain from your neighbors by extortion. And you have forgotten me, declares the Sovereign LORD.

Ezekiel 22:12

Jesus said to him, "Away from me, Satan! For it is written: 'Worship the Lord your God, and serve him only.'"

Matthew 4:10

Do not store up for yourselves treasures on earth, where moth and rust destroy, and where thieves break in and steal. But store up for yourselves treasures in heaven, where moth and rust do not destroy, and where thieves do not break in and steal. For where your treasure is, there your heart will be also.

Matthew 6:19-21

No one can serve two masters. Either he will hate the one and love the other, or he will be devoted to the one and despise the other. You cannot serve both God and Money. Therefore I tell you, do not worry about your life, what you will eat or drink; or about your body, what you will wear. Is not life more important than food, and the body more important than clothes? Look at the birds of the air; they do not sow or reap or store away in barns, and yet your heavenly Father feeds them. Are you not much more valuable than they? Who of you by worrying can add a single hour to his life? And why do you worry about clothes? See how the lilies of the field grow. They do not labor or spin. Yet I tell you that not even Solomon in all his splendor was dressed like one of these. If that is how God clothes the grass of the field, which is here today and tomorrow is thrown into the fire, will he not much more clothe you, O you of little faith? So do not worry, saying, What shall we eat? or What shall we drink? or What shall we wear? For the pagans run after all these things, and your heavenly Father knows that you need them. But seek first his kingdom and his righteousness, and all these things will be given to you as well.

Matthew 6:24-33

Jesus answered, "It is written: 'Worship the Lord your God and serve him only.'"

Luke 4:8

Then he said to them, "Watch out! Be on your guard against all kinds of greed; a man's life does not consist in the abundance of his possessions." And he told them this parable: "The ground of a certain rich man produced a good crop. He thought to himself, 'What shall I do? I have no place to store my crops.' "Then he said, 'This is what I'll do. I will tear down my barns and build bigger ones, and there I will store all my grain and my goods. And I'll say to myself, "You have plenty of good things laid up for many years. Take life easy; eat, drink and be merry."' "But God said to him, 'You fool! This very night your life will be demanded from you. Then who will get what you have prepared for yourself?' "This is how it will be with anyone who stores up things for himself but is not rich toward God."

Luke 12:15-21

Put to death, therefore, whatever belongs to your earthly nature: sexual immorality, impurity, lust, evil desires and greed, which is idolatry.

Colossians 3:5

For the love of money is a root of all kinds of evil. Some people, eager for money, have wandered from the faith and pierced themselves with many griefs. But you, man of God, flee from all this, and pursue righteousness, godliness, faith, love, endurance and gentleness.

1 Timothy 6:10-11

Command those who are rich in this present world not to be arrogant nor to put their hope in wealth, which is so uncertain, but to put their hope in God, who richly provides us with everything for our enjoyment. Command them to do good, to be rich in good deeds, and to be generous and willing to share. In this way they will lay up treasure for themselves as a firm foundation for the coming age, so that they may take hold of the life that is truly life.

1 Timothy 6:17-19

But mark this: There will be terrible times in the last days. People will be lovers of themselves, lovers of money, boastful, proud, abusive, disobedient to their parents, ungrateful, unholy, without love, unforgiving, slanderous, without self-control, brutal, not lovers of the good, treacherous, rash, conceited, lovers of pleasure rather than lovers of God — having a form of godliness but denying its power. Have nothing to do with them.

2 Timothy 3:1-5

Do not love the world or anything in the world. If anyone loves the world, the love of the Father is not in him. For everything in the world — the cravings of sinful man, the lust of his eyes and the boasting of what he has and does — comes not from the Father but from the world. The world and its desires pass away, but the man who does the will of God lives forever.

1 John 2:15-17

Stewardship @ Work

Love of Money @ Work

In the beginning God created the heavens and the earth.

Genesis 1:1

Then God said, "Let us make man in our image, in our likeness, and let them rule over the fish of the sea and the birds of the air, over the livestock, over all the earth, and over all the creatures that move along the ground." So God created man in his own image, in the image of God he created him; male and female he created them. God blessed them and said to them, "Be fruitful and increase in number; fill the earth and subdue it. Rule over the fish of the sea and the birds of the air and over every living creature that moves on the ground." Then God said, "I give you every seed-bearing plant on the face of the whole earth and every tree that has fruit with seed in it. They will be yours for food. And to all the beasts of the earth and all the birds of the air and all the creatures that move on the ground — everything that has the breath of life in it — I give every green plant for food." And it was so.

Genesis 1:26-30

Moses replied, "When I have gone out of the city, I will spread out my hands in prayer to the LORD. The thunder will stop and there will be no more hail, so you may know that the earth is the LORD's."

Exodus 9:29

For in six days the LORD made the heavens and the earth, the sea, and all that is in them, but he rested on the seventh day.

Exodus 20:11

To the LORD your God belong the heavens, even the highest heavens, the earth and everything in it.

Deuteronomy 10:14

David praised the LORD in the presence of the whole assembly, saying, "Praise be to you, O LORD, God of our father Israel, from everlasting to everlasting. Yours, O LORD, is the greatness and the power and the glory and the majesty and the splendor, for everything in heaven and earth is yours. Yours, O LORD, is the kingdom; you are exalted as head over all. Wealth and honor come from you; you are the ruler of all things. In your hands are strength and power to exalt and give strength to all. Now, our God, we give you thanks, and praise your glorious name."

1 Chronicles 29:10-13

You alone are the LORD. You made the heavens, even the highest heavens, and all their starry host, the earth and all that is on it, the seas and all that is in them. You give life to everything, and the multitudes of heaven worship you.

Nehemiah 9:6

When I consider your heavens, the work of your fingers, the moon and the stars, which you have set in place, what is man that you are mindful of him, the son of man that you care for him? You made him a little lower than the heavenly beings and crowned him with glory and honor. You made him ruler over the works of your hands; you put everything under his feet: all flocks and herds, and the beasts of the field, the birds of the air, and the fish of the sea, all that swim the paths of the seas. O LORD, our Lord, how majestic is your name in all the earth!

Psalm 8:3-9

The earth is the LORD's, and everything in it, the world, and all who live in it;

Psalm 24:1

Hear, O my people, and I will speak, O Israel, and I will testify against you: I am God, your God. I do not rebuke you for your sacrifices or your burnt offerings, which are ever before me. I have no need of a bull from your stall or of goats from your pens, for every animal of the forest is mine, and the cattle on a thousand hills. I know every bird in the mountains, and the creatures of the field are mine. If I were hungry I would not tell you, for the world is mine, and all that is in it.

Psalm 50:7-12

The heavens are yours, and yours also the earth; you founded the world and all that is in it.

Psalm 89:11

Know that the LORD is God. It is he who made us, and we are his; we are his people, the sheep of his pasture.

Psalm 100:3

May you be blessed by the LORD, the Maker of heaven and earth. The highest heavens belong to the LORD, but the earth he has given to man.

Psalm 115:15-16

Our help is in the name of the LORD, the Maker of heaven and earth.

Psalm 124:8

O LORD Almighty, God of Israel, enthroned between the cherubim, you alone are God over all the kingdoms of the earth. You have made heaven and earth.

Isaiah 37:16

For this is what the LORD says — he who created the heavens, he is God; he who fashioned and made the earth, he founded it; he did not create it to be empty, but formed it to be inhabited — he says: "I am the LORD, and there is no other."

Isaiah 45:18

Who then is the faithful and wise servant, whom the master has put in charge of the servants in his household to give them their food at the proper time? It will be good for that servant whose master finds him doing so when he returns. I tell you the truth, he will put him in charge of all his possessions.

Matthew 24:45-47

"Again, it will be like a man going on a journey, who called his servants and entrusted his property to them. To one he gave five talents of money, to another two talents, and to another one talent, each according to his ability. Then he went on his journey. The man who had received the five talents went at once and put his money to work and gained five more. So also, the one with the two talents gained two more. But the man who had received the one talent went off, dug a hole in the ground and hid his master's money. "After a long time the master of those servants returned and settled accounts with them. The man who had received the five talents brought the other five. 'Master,' he said, 'you entrusted me with five talents. See, I have gained five more.' "His master replied, 'Well done, good and faithful servant! You have been faithful with a few things; I will put you in charge of many things. Come and share your master's happiness!' "The man with the two talents also came. 'Master,' he said, 'you entrusted me with two talents; see, I have gained two more.' "His master replied, 'Well done, good and faithful servant! You have been faithful with a few things; I will put you in charge of many things. Come and share your master's happiness!' "Then the man who had received the one talent came. 'Master,' he said, 'I knew that you are a hard man, harvesting where you have not sown and gathering where you have not scattered seed. So I was afraid and went out and hid your talent in the ground. See, here is what belongs to you.' "His master replied, 'You wicked, lazy servant! So you knew that I harvest where I have not sown and gather where I have not scattered seed? Well then, you should have put my money on deposit with the bankers, so that when I returned I would have received it back with interest. "'Take the talent from him and give it to the one who has the ten talents. For everyone who has will be given more, and he will have an abundance. Whoever does not have, even what he has will be taken from him. And throw that worthless servant outside, into the darkness, where there will be weeping and gnashing of teeth.'"

Matthew 25:14-30

From everyone who has been given much, much will be demanded; and from the one who has been entrusted with much, much more will be asked.

Luke 12:48

Whoever can be trusted with very little can also be trusted with much, and whoever is dishonest with very little will also be dishonest with much. So if you have not been trustworthy in handling worldly wealth, who will trust you with true riches? And if you have not been trustworthy with someone else's property, who will give you property of your own?

Luke 16:10-12

For none of us lives to himself alone and none of us dies to himself alone. If we live, we live to the Lord; and if we die, we die to the Lord. So, whether we live or die, we belong to the Lord.

Romans 14:7-8

Moreover it is required in stewards, that a man be found faithful.

1 Corinthians 4:2 (KJV)

Do you not know that your body is a temple of the Holy Spirit, who is in you, whom you have received from God? You are not your own; you were bought at a price. Therefore honor God with your body.

1 Corinthians 6:19-20

For, the earth is the Lord's, and everything in it.

1 Corinthians 10:26

You are worthy, our Lord and God, to receive glory and honor and power, for you created all things, and by your will they were created and have their being.

Revelation 4:11

Borrowing and Lending @ Work

Love of Money @ Work

If a man borrows an animal from his neighbor and it is injured or dies while the owner is not present, he must make restitution. But if the owner is with the animal, the borrower will not have to pay. If the animal was hired, the money paid for the hire covers the loss.

Exodus 22:14-15

At the end of every seven years you must cancel debts. This is how it is to be done: Every creditor shall cancel the loan he has made to his fellow Israelite. He shall not require payment from his fellow Israelite or brother, because the LORD's time for canceling debts has been proclaimed. You may require payment from a foreigner, but you must cancel any debt your brother owes you. However, there should be no poor among you, for in the land the LORD your God is giving you to possess as your inheritance, he will richly bless you, if only you fully obey the LORD your God and are careful to follow all these commands I am giving you today. For the LORD your God will bless you as he has promised, and you will lend to many nations but will borrow from none. You will rule over many nations but none will rule over you. If there is a poor man among your brothers in any of the towns of the land that the LORD your God is giving you, do not be hardhearted or tightfisted toward your poor brother. Rather be openhanded and freely lend him whatever he needs. Be careful not to harbor this wicked thought: The seventh year, the year for canceling debts, is near, so that you do not show ill will toward your needy brother and give him nothing. He may then appeal to the LORD against you, and you will be found guilty of sin. Give generously to him and do so without a grudging heart; then because of this the LORD your God will bless you in all your work and in everything you put your hand to.

Deuteronomy 15:1-10

Do not charge your brother interest, whether on money or food or anything else that may earn interest. You may charge a foreigner interest, but not a brother Israelite, so that the LORD your God may bless you in everything you put your hand to in the land you are entering to possess.

Deuteronomy 23:19-20

If you fully obey the LORD your God and carefully follow all his commands I give you today, the LORD your God will set you high above all the nations on earth. All these blessings will come upon you and accompany you if you obey the LORD your God: You will be blessed in the city and blessed in the country. The fruit of your womb will be blessed, and the crops of your land and the young of your livestock — the calves of your herds and the lambs of your flocks. Your basket and your kneading trough will be blessed. You will be blessed when you come in and blessed when you go out. The LORD will grant that the enemies who rise up against you will be defeated before you. They will come at you from one direction but flee from you in seven. The LORD will send a blessing on your barns and on everything you put your hand to. The LORD your God will bless you in the land he is giving you. The LORD will establish you as his holy people, as he promised you on oath, if you keep the commands of the LORD your God and walk in his ways. Then all the peoples on earth will see that you are called by the name of the LORD, and they will fear you. The LORD will grant you abundant prosperity — in the fruit of your womb, the young of your livestock and the crops of your ground — in the land he swore to your forefathers to give you. The LORD will open the heavens, the storehouse of his bounty, to send rain on your land in season and to bless all the work of your hands. You will lend to many nations but will borrow from none.

Deuteronomy 28:1-12

However, if you do not obey the LORD your God and do not carefully follow all his commands and decrees I am giving you today, all these curses will come upon you and overtake you: You will be cursed in the city and cursed in the country. Your basket and your kneading trough will be cursed. The fruit of your womb will be cursed, and the crops of your land, and the calves of your herds and the lambs of your flocks. You will be cursed when you come in and cursed when you go out.

Deuteronomy 28:15-19

The alien who lives among you will rise above you higher and higher, but you will sink lower and lower. He will lend to you, but you will not lend to him. He will be the head, but you will be the tail.

Deuteronomy 28: 43-44

The wife of a man from the company of the prophets cried out to Elisha, "Your servant my husband is dead, and you know that he revered the LORD. But now his creditor is coming to take my two boys as his slaves." Elisha replied to her, "How can I help you? Tell me, what do you have in your house?" "Your servant has nothing there at all," she said, "except a little oil." Elisha said, "Go around and ask all your neighbors for empty jars. Don't ask for just a few. Then go inside and shut the door behind you and your sons. Pour oil into all the jars, and as each is filled, put it to one side." She left him and afterward shut the door behind her and her sons. They brought the jars to her and she kept pouring. When all the jars were full, she said to her son, "Bring me another one." But he replied, "There is not a jar left." Then the oil stopped flowing. She went and told the man of God, and he said, "Go, sell the oil and pay your debts. You and your sons can live on what is left."

2 Kings 4:1-7

The wicked borrow and do not repay, but the righteous give generously.

Psalm 37:21

I was young and now I am old, yet I have never seen the righteous forsaken or their children begging bread. They are always generous and lend freely; their children will be blessed.

Psalm 37:25-25

Good will come to him who is generous and lends freely, who conducts his affairs with justice.

Psalm 112:5

Do not withhold good from those who deserve it, when it is in your power to act. Do not say to your neighbor, Come back later; I'll give it tomorrow — when you now have it with you.

Proverbs 3:27-28

One man gives freely, yet gains even more; another withholds unduly, but comes to poverty. A generous man will prosper; he who refreshes others will himself be refreshed.

Proverbs 11:24-25

There is a way that seems right to a man, but in the end it leads to death.

Proverbs 14:12

The rich rule over the poor, and the borrower is servant to the lender.

Proverbs 22:7

Give to the one who asks you, and do not turn away from the one who wants to borrow from you.

Matthew 5:42

But love your enemies, do good to them, and lend to them without expecting to get anything back. Then your reward will be great, and you will be sons of the Most High, because he is kind to the ungrateful and wicked.

Luke 6:35

Suppose one of you wants to build a tower. Will he not first sit down and estimate the cost to see if he has enough money to complete it? For if he lays the foundation and is not able to finish it, everyone who sees it will ridicule him,

Luke 14:28-29

Whoever can be trusted with very little can also be trusted with much, and whoever is dishonest with very little will also be dishonest with much. So if you have not been trustworthy in handling worldly wealth, who will trust you with true riches? And if you have not been trustworthy with someone else's property, who will give you property of your own? No servant can serve two masters. Either he will hate the one and love the other, or he will be devoted to the one and despise the other. You cannot serve both God and Money.

Luke 16:10-13

Let no debt remain outstanding, except the continuing debt to love one another, for he who loves his fellowman has fulfilled the law.

Romans 13:8

And my God will meet all your needs according to his glorious riches in Christ Jesus.

Philippians 4:19

Interest (Usury) @ Work

Love of Money @ Work

If you lend money to one of my people among you who is needy, do not be like a moneylender; charge him no interest. If you take your neighbor's cloak as a pledge, return it to him by sunset, because his cloak is the only covering he has for his body. What else will he sleep in? When he cries out to me, I will hear, for I am compassionate.

Exodus 22:25-27

If one of your countrymen becomes poor and is unable to support himself among you, help him as you would an alien or a temporary resident, so he can continue to live among you. Do not take interest of any kind from him, but fear your God, so that your countryman may continue to live among you. You must not lend him money at interest or sell him food at a profit.

Leviticus 25:35-37

Do not charge your brother interest, whether on money or food or anything else that may earn interest. You may charge a foreigner interest, but not a brother Israelite, so that the LORD your God may bless you in everything you put your hand to in the land you are entering to possess.

Deuteronomy 23:19-20

Now the men and their wives raised a great outcry against their Jewish brothers. Some were saying, "We and our sons and daughters are numerous; in order for us to eat and stay alive, we must get grain." Others were saying, "We are mortgaging our fields, our vineyards and our homes to get grain during the famine." Still others were saying, "We have had to borrow money to pay the king's tax on our fields and vineyards. Although we are of the same flesh and blood as our countrymen and though our sons are as good as theirs, yet we have to subject our sons and daughters to slavery. Some of our daughters have already been enslaved, but we are powerless, because our fields and our vineyards belong to others." When I heard their outcry and these charges, I was very angry. I pondered them in my mind and then accused the nobles and officials. I told them, "You are exacting usury from your own countrymen!" So I called together a large meeting to deal with them and said: "As far as possible, we have bought back our Jewish brothers who were sold to the Gentiles. Now you are selling your brothers, only for them to be sold back to us!" They kept quiet, because they could find nothing to say. So I continued, "What you are doing is not right. Shouldn't you walk in the fear of our God to avoid the reproach of our Gentile enemies? I and my brothers and my men are also lending the people money and grain. But let the exacting of usury stop!"

Nehemiah 5:1-10

LORD, who may dwell in your sanctuary? Who may live on your holy hill? He whose walk is blameless and who does what is righteous, who speaks the truth from his heart and has no slander on his tongue, who does his neighbor no wrong and casts no slur on his fellowman, who despises a vile man but honors those who fear the LORD, who keeps his oath even when it hurts, who lends his money without usury and does not accept a bribe against the innocent. He who does these things will never be shaken.

Psalm 15:1-5

He who increases his wealth by exorbitant interest amasses it for another, who will be kind to the poor.

Proverbs 28:8

Suppose there is a righteous man who does what is just and right. He does not eat at the mountain shrines or look to the idols of the house of

Israel. He does not defile his neighbor's wife or lie with a woman during her period. He does not oppress anyone, but returns what he took in pledge for a loan. He does not commit robbery but gives his food to the hungry and provides clothing for the naked. He does not lend at usury or take excessive interest. He withholds his hand from doing wrong and judges fairly between man and man. He follows my decrees and faithfully keeps my laws. That man is righteous; he will surely live, declares the Sovereign LORD.

                                                        Ezekiel 18:5-9

Surety (Co-Signing) for Debts @ Work

If you take your neighbor's cloak as a pledge, return it to him by sunset, because his cloak is the only covering he has for his body. What else will he sleep in? When he cries out to me, I will hear, for I am compassionate.

Exodus 22:26-27

When you make a loan of any kind to your neighbor, do not go into his house to get what he is offering as a pledge. Stay outside and let the man to whom you are making the loan bring the pledge out to you. If the man is poor, do not go to sleep with his pledge in your possession. Return his cloak to him by sunset so that he may sleep in it. Then he will thank you, and it will be regarded as a righteous act in the sight of the LORD your God.

Deuteronomy 24:10-13

My son, if you have put up security for your neighbor, if you have struck hands in pledge for another, if you have been trapped by what you said, ensnared by the words of your mouth, then do this, my son, to free yourself, since you have fallen into your neighbor's hands: Go and humble yourself; press your plea with your neighbor! Allow no sleep to your eyes, no slumber to your eyelids. Free yourself, like a gazelle from the hand of the hunter, like a bird from the snare of the fowler.

Proverbs 6:1-5

He who puts up security for another will surely suffer, but whoever refuses to strike hands in pledge is safe.

> Proverbs 11:15

A man lacking in judgment strikes hands in pledge and puts up security for his neighbor.

> Proverbs 17:18

Do not be a man who strikes hands in pledge or puts up security for debts; if you lack the means to pay, your very bed will be snatched from under you.

> Proverbs 22:26-27

Take the garment of one who puts up security for a stranger; hold it in pledge if he does it for a wayward woman.

> Proverbs 27:13

"Suppose there is a righteous man who does what is just and right. He does not eat at the mountain shrines or look to the idols of the house of Israel. He does not defile his neighbor's wife or lie with a woman during her period. He does not oppress anyone, but returns what he took in pledge for a loan. He does not commit robbery but gives his food to the hungry and provides clothing for the naked. He does not lend at usury or take excessive interest. He withholds his hand from doing wrong and judges fairly between man and man. He follows my decrees and faithfully keeps my laws. That man is righteous; he will surely live," declares the Sovereign LORD.

> Ezekiel 18:5-9

Love of Money @ Work

Do not defraud your neighbor or rob him. Do not hold back the wages of a hired man overnight.

Leviticus 19:13

Do not take advantage of a hired man who is poor and needy, whether he is a brother Israelite or an alien living in one of your towns. Pay him his wages each day before sunset, because he is poor and is counting on it. Otherwise he may cry to the LORD against you, and you will be guilty of sin.

Deuteronomy 24:14-15

If I have denied justice to my menservants and maidservants when they had a grievance against me, what will I do when God confronts me? What will I answer when called to account? Did not he who made me in the womb make them? Did not the same one form us both within our mothers?

Job 31:13-15

Do not say to your neighbor, "Come back later; I'll give it tomorrow" — when you now have it with you.

Proverbs 3:28

The wages of the righteous bring them life, but the income of the wicked brings them punishment.

Proverbs 10:16

The LORD abhors dishonest scales, but accurate weights are his delight.

Proverbs 11:1

The wicked man earns deceptive wages, but he who sows righteousness reaps a sure reward.

Proverbs 11:18

A generous man will prosper; he who refreshes others will himself be refreshed.

Proverbs 11:25

All hard work brings a profit, but mere talk leads only to poverty.

Proverbs 14:23

He who oppresses the poor shows contempt for their Maker, but whoever is kind to the needy honors God.

Proverbs 14: 31

Better a little with the fear of the LORD than great wealth with turmoil.

Proverbs 15:16

A wise servant (employee) will rule over a disgraceful son, and will share the inheritance as one of the brothers.

Proverbs 17:2

Differing weights and differing measures — the LORD detests them both.

Proverbs 20:10

The LORD detests differing weights, and dishonest scales do not please him.

Proverbs 20:23

To do what is right and just is more acceptable to the LORD than sacrifice.

Proverbs 21:3

A fortune made by a lying tongue is a fleeting vapor and a deadly snare.

Proverbs 21:6

Woe to him who builds his palace by unrighteousness, his upper rooms by injustice, making his countrymen work for nothing, not paying them for their labor.

Jeremiah 22:13

"So I will come near to you for judgment. I will be quick to testify against sorcerers, adulterers and perjurers, against those who defraud laborers of their wages, who oppress the widows and the fatherless, and deprive aliens of justice, but do not fear me," says the LORD Almighty.

Malachi 3:5

For the worker is worth his keep.

Matthew 10:10

The second is this: Love your neighbor as yourself. There is no commandment greater than these.

Mark 12:31

"For the kingdom of heaven is like a landowner who went out early in the morning to hire men to work in his vineyard. He agreed to pay them a denarius for the day and sent them into his vineyard. "About the third hour he went out and saw others standing in the marketplace doing nothing. He told them, 'You also go and work in my vineyard, and I will pay you whatever is right.' So they went. "He went out again about the sixth hour and the ninth hour and did the same thing. About the eleventh hour he went out and found still others standing around. He asked them, 'Why have you been standing here all day long doing nothing?' "'Because no one has hired us,' they answered. "He said to them, 'You also go and work in my vineyard.' "When evening came, the owner of the vineyard said to his foreman, 'Call the workers and pay them their wages, beginning with the last ones hired and going on to the first.'

"The workers who were hired about the eleventh hour came and each received a denarius. So when those came who were hired first, they expected to receive more. But each one of them also received a denarius.

When they received it, they began to grumble against the landowner. 'These men who were hired last worked only one hour,' they said, 'and you have made them equal to us who have borne the burden of the work and the heat of the day.'

"But he answered one of them, 'Friend, I am not being unfair to you. Didn't you agree to work for a denarius? Take your pay and go. I want to give the man who was hired last the same as I gave you. Don't I have the right to do what I want with my own money? Or are you envious because I am generous?' "So the last will be first, and the first will be last."

Matthew 20:1-16

Tax collectors also came to be baptized. "Teacher," they asked, "what should we do?" "Don't collect any more than you are required to," he told them. Then some soldiers asked him, "And what should we do?" He replied, "Don't extort money and don't accuse people falsely — be content with your pay."

Luke 3:12-14

Who serves as a soldier at his own expense? Who plants a vineyard and does not eat of its grapes? Who tends a flock and does not drink of the milk? Do I say this merely from a human point of view? Doesn't the Law say the same thing? For it is written in the Law of Moses: "Do not muzzle an ox while it is treading out the grain." Is it about oxen that God is concerned? Surely he says this for us, doesn't he? Yes, this was written for us, because when the plowman plows and the thresher threshes, they ought to do so in the hope of sharing in the harvest.

1 Corinthians 9:7-10

Do nothing out of selfish ambition or vain conceit, but in humility consider others better than yourselves. Each of you should look not only to your own interests, but also to the interests of others.

Philippians 2:3-4

Masters (employers), provide your slaves (employees) with what is right and fair, because you know that you also have a Master in heaven.

Colossians 4:1

For the Scripture says, "Do not muzzle the ox while it is treading out the grain," and "The worker deserves his wages."

1 Timothy 5:18

Command those who are rich in this present world not to be arrogant nor to put their hope in wealth, which is so uncertain, but to put their hope in God, who richly provides us with everything for our enjoyment. Command them to do good, to be rich in good deeds, and to be generous and willing to share. In this way they will lay up treasure for themselves as a firm foundation for the coming age, so that they may take hold of the life that is truly life.

1 Timothy 6:17-19

Now listen, you rich people, weep and wail because of the misery that is coming upon you. Your wealth has rotted, and moths have eaten your clothes. Your gold and silver are corroded. Their corrosion will testify against you and eat your flesh like fire. You have hoarded wealth in the last days. Look! The wages you failed to pay the workmen who mowed your fields are crying out against you. The cries of the harvesters have reached the ears of the Lord Almighty.

James 5:1-4

Love of Money @ Work

Blessed are they who maintain justice, who constantly do what is right.

Psalm 106:3

Let your eyes look straight ahead, fix your gaze directly before you. Make level paths for your feet and take only ways that are firm. Do not swerve to the right or the left; keep your foot from evil.

Proverbs 4:25-27

The man of integrity walks securely, but he who takes crooked paths will be found out.

Proverbs 10:9

The integrity of the upright guides them, but the unfaithful are destroyed by their duplicity.

Proverbs 11:3

The LORD detests lying lips, but he delights in men who are truthful.

Proverbs 12:22

What a man desires is unfailing love; better to be poor than a liar.

Proverbs 19:22

To do what is right and just is more acceptable to the LORD than sacrifice.

Proverbs 21:3

He who walks righteously and speaks what is right, who rejects gain from extortion and keeps his hand from accepting bribes, who stops his ears against plots of murder and shuts his eyes against contemplating evil — this is the man who will dwell on the heights, whose refuge will be the mountain fortress. His bread will be supplied, and water will not fail him.

Isaiah 33:15-16

After Jesus and his disciples arrived in Capernaum, the collectors of the two-drachma tax came to Peter and asked, "Doesn't your teacher pay the temple tax?" "Yes, he does," he replied. When Peter came into the house, Jesus was the first to speak. "What do you think, Simon?" He asked. "From whom do the kings of the earth collect duty and taxes — from their own sons or from others?" "From others," Peter answered. "Then the sons are exempt," Jesus said to him. "But so that we may not offend them, go to the lake and throw out your line. Take the first fish you catch; open its mouth and you will find a four-drachma coin. Take it and give it to them for my tax and yours."

Matthew 17:24-27

"Tell us then, what is your opinion? Is it right to pay taxes to Caesar or not?" But Jesus, knowing their evil intent, said, "You hypocrites, why are you trying to trap me? Show me the coin used for paying the tax." They brought him a denarius, and he asked them, "Whose portrait is this? And whose inscription?" "Caesar's," they replied. Then he said to them, "Give to Caesar what is Caesar's, and to God what is God's."

Matthew 22:17-21

They came to him and said, "Teacher, we know you are a man of integrity. You aren't swayed by men, because you pay no attention to who they are; but you teach the way of God in accordance with the truth. Is it right to pay taxes to Caesar or not? Should we pay or shouldn't we?" But Jesus knew their hypocrisy. "Why are you trying to trap me?" He asked. "Bring me a denarius and let me look at it." They brought the coin, and he asked them, "Whose portrait is this? And whose inscription?" "Caesar's," they replied. Then Jesus said to them, "Give to Caesar what is Caesar's and to God what is God's." And they were amazed at him.

Mark 12:14-17

There is nothing concealed that will not be disclosed, or hidden that will not be made known. What you have said in the dark will be heard in the daylight, and what you have whispered in the ear in the inner rooms will be proclaimed from the roofs.

Luke 12:2-3

Everyone must submit himself to the governing authorities, for there is no authority except that which God has established. The authorities that exist have been established by God. Consequently, he who rebels against the authority is rebelling against what God has instituted, and those who do so will bring judgment on themselves. For rulers hold no terror for those who do right, but for those who do wrong. Do you want to be free from fear of the one in authority? Then do what is right and he will commend you. For he is God's servant to do you good. But if you do wrong, be afraid, for he does not bear the sword for nothing. He is God's servant, an agent of wrath to bring punishment on the wrongdoer. Therefore, it is necessary to submit to the authorities, not only because of possible punishment but also because of conscience. This is also why you pay taxes, for the authorities are God's servants, who give their full time to governing. Give everyone what you owe him: If you owe taxes, pay taxes; if revenue, then revenue; if respect, then respect; if honor, then honor. Let no debt remain outstanding, except the continuing debt to love one another, for he who loves his fellowman has fulfilled the law.

Romans 13:1-8

Rather, we have renounced secret and shameful ways; we do not use deception, nor do we distort the word of God. On the contrary, by setting forth the truth plainly we commend ourselves to every man's conscience in the sight of God.

2 Corinthians 4:2

So we make it our goal to please him, whether we are at home in the body or away from it. For we must all appear before the judgment seat of Christ, that each one may receive what is due him for the things done while in the body, whether good or bad.

2 Corinthians 5:9-10

For we are taking pains to do what is right, not only in the eyes of the Lord but also in the eyes of men.

2 Corinthians 8:21

Live such good lives among the pagans that, though they accuse you of doing wrong, they may see your good deeds and glorify God on the day he visits us.

1 Peter 2:12

Keeping a clear conscience, so that those who speak maliciously against your good behavior in Christ may be ashamed of their slander.

1 Peter 3:16

Bribes @ Work

Do not accept a bribe, for a bribe blinds those who see and twists the words of the righteous.

Exodus 23:8

Do not pervert justice or show partiality. Do not accept a bribe, for a bribe blinds the eyes of the wise and twists the words of the righteous. Follow justice and justice alone, so that you may live and possess the land the LORD your God is giving you.

Deuteronomy 16:19-20

Cursed is the man who accepts a bribe to kill an innocent person. Then all the people shall say, Amen!

Deuteronomy 27:25

For the company of the godless will be barren, and fire will consume the tents of those who love bribes.

Job 15:34

A greedy man brings trouble to his family, but he who hates bribes tears it down.

Proverbs 15:27

A wicked man accepts a bribe in secret to pervert the course of justice.

Proverbs 17:23

By justice a king gives a country stability, but one who is greedy for bribes tears it down.

Proverbs 29:4

Extortion turns a wise man into a fool, and a bribe corrupts the heart.

Ecclesiastes 7:7

Woe to those who are heroes at drinking wine and champions at mixing drinks, who acquit the guilty for a bribe, but deny justice to the innocent.

Isaiah 5:22-23

He who walks righteously and speaks what is right, who rejects gain from extortion and keeps his hand from accepting bribes, who stops his ears against plots of murder and shuts his eyes against contemplating evil — this is the man who will dwell on the heights, whose refuge will be the mountain fortress. His bread will be supplied, and water will not fail him.

Isaiah 33:15-16

In you men accept bribes to shed blood; you take usury and excessive interest and make unjust gain from your neighbors by extortion. And you have forgotten me, declares the Sovereign LORD.

Ezekiel 22:12

Part Two

Godly Character @ Work

Character @ Work

Godly Character @ Work

A good name is more desirable than great riches; to be esteemed is better than silver or gold.

Proverbs 22:1

A good name is better than fine perfume, and the day of death better than the day of birth.

Ecclesiastes 7:1

Therefore, since we have been justified through faith, we have peace with God through our Lord Jesus Christ, through whom we have gained access by faith into this grace in which we now stand. And we rejoice in the hope of the glory of God. Not only so, but we also rejoice in our sufferings, because we know that suffering produces perseverance; character; and character, hope.

Romans 5:1-4

So whether you eat or drink or whatever you do, do it all for the glory of God.

1 Corinthians 10:31

But the fruit of the Spirit is love, joy, peace, patience, kindness, goodness, faithfulness, gentleness and self-control. Against such things there is no law.

Galatians 5:22-23

77

As a prisoner for the Lord, then, I urge you to live a life worthy of the calling you have received. Be completely humble and gentle; be patient, bearing with one another in love. Make every effort to keep the unity of the Spirit through the bond of peace.

Ephesians 4:1-3

Be imitators of God, therefore, as dearly loved children

Ephesians 5:1

Slaves (employees), obey your earthly master (employers) with respect and fear, and with sincerity of heart, just as you would obey Christ. Obey them not only to win their favor when their eye is on you, but like slaves of Christ, doing the will of God from your heart.. Serve whole-heartedly, as if you were serving the Lord, not men, because you know that the Lord will reward everyone for whatever good he does, whether he is slave or free. And masters, treat your slaves in the same way. Do not threaten them, since you know that he who is both their Master and yours is in heaven, and there is no favoritism with him.

Ephesians 6:5-9

And whatever you do, whether in word or deed, do it all in the name of the Lord Jesus, giving thanks to God the Father through him.

Colossians 3:17

Slaves (employees), obey your earthly masters (employers) in every-thing; and do it, not only when their eye is on you and to win their favor, but with sincerity of heart and reverence for the Lord. Whatever you do, work at it with all your heart, as working for the Lord, not for men, since you know that you will receive an inheritance from the Lord as a reward. It is the Lord Christ you are serving.

Colossians 3:22-24

But you, man of God, flee from all this, and pursue righteousness, god-liness, faith, love, endurance and gentleness.

1 Timothy 6:11

Teach the older men to be temperate, worthy of respect, self-controlled, and sound in faith, in love and in endurance. Likewise, teach the older women to be reverent in the way they live, not to be slanderers or addicted to much wine, but to teach what is good. Then they can train the younger women to love their husbands and children, to be self-controlled and pure, to be busy at home, to be kind, and to be subject to their husbands, so that no one will malign the word of God. Similarly, encourage the young men to be self-controlled. In everything set them an example by doing what is good. In your teaching show integrity, seriousness and soundness of speech that cannot be condemned, so that those who oppose you may be ashamed because they have nothing bad to say about us.

Teach slaves (employees) to be subject to their masters (employers) in everything, to try to please them, not to talk back to them, and not to steal from them, but to show that they can be fully trusted, so that in every way they will make the teaching about God our Savior attractive. For the grace of God that brings salvation has appeared to all men. It teaches us to say No to ungodliness and worldly passions, and to live self-controlled, upright and godly lives in this present age, while we wait for the blessed hope — the glorious appearing of our great God and Savior, Jesus Christ, who gave himself for us to redeem us from all wickedness and to purify for himself a people that are his very own, eager to do what is good.

Titus 2:2-14

Remind the people to be subject to rulers and authorities, to be obedient, to be ready to do whatever is good, to slander no one, to be peaceable and considerate, and to show true humility toward all men.

Titus 3:1-2

For this very reason, make every effort to add to your faith goodness; and to goodness, knowledge; and to knowledge, self-control; and to self-control, perseverance; and to perseverance, godliness; and to godliness, brotherly kindness; and to brotherly kindness, love. For if you possess these qualities in increasing measure, they will keep you from being ineffective and unproductive in your knowledge of our Lord Jesus Christ. But if anyone does not have them, he is near sighted and blind, and has forgotten that he has been cleansed from his past sins.

2 Peter 1:5-9

Integrity @ Work

Godly Character @ Work

For I have chosen him, so that he will direct his children and his household after him to keep the way of the LORD by doing what is right and just, so that the LORD will bring about for Abraham what he has promised him.

Genesis 18:19

But select capable men from all the people — men who fear God, trustworthy men who hate dishonest gain — and appoint them as officials over thousands, hundreds, fifties and tens.

Exodus 18:21

Do not steal. Do not lie. Do not deceive one another.

Leviticus 19:11

Do not pervert justice or show partiality. Do not accept a bribe, for a bribe blinds the eyes of the wise and twists the words of the righteous. Follow justice and justice alone, so that you may live and possess the land the LORD your God is giving you.

Deuteronomy 16:19-20

Do not have two differing weights in your bag — one heavy, one light. Do not have two differing measures in your house — one large, one small. You must have accurate and honest weights and measures, so that you may live long in the land the LORD your God is giving you. For the LORD your God detests anyone who does these things, anyone who deals dishonestly.

Deuteronomy 25:13-16

The LORD has dealt with me according to my righteousness; according to the cleanness of my hands he has rewarded me.

2 Samuel 22:21

I put in charge of Jerusalem my brother Hanani, along with Hananiah the commander of the citadel, because he was a man of integrity and feared God more than most men do.

Nehemiah 7:2

My lips will not speak wickedness, and my tongue will utter no deceit. I will never admit you are in the right; till I die, I will not deny my integrity. I will maintain my righteousness and never let go of it; my conscience will not reproach me as long as I live.

Job 27:4-6

I put on righteousness as my clothing; justice was my robe and my turban.

Job 29:14

I made a covenant with my eyes not to look lustfully at a girl. For what is man's lot from God above, his heritage from the Almighty on high? Is it not ruin for the wicked, disaster for those who do wrong? Does he not see my ways and count my every step? If I have walked in falsehood or my foot has hurried after deceit — let God weigh me in honest scales and he will know that I am blameless — if my steps have turned from the path, if my heart has been led by my eyes, or if my hands have been defiled, then may others eat what I have sown, and may my crops be uprooted. If my heart has been enticed by a woman, or if I have lurked at my neighbor's door, then may my wife grind another man's grain, and may other men sleep with her. For that would have been shameful, a sin to be judged. It is a fire that burns to Destruction; it would have uprooted my harvest. If I have denied justice to my menservants and maidservants when they had a grievance against me, what will I do when God confronts me? What will I answer when called to account? Did not he who made me in the womb make them? Did not the same one form us both within our mothers? If I have denied the desires of the poor or let the eyes of the widow grow weary, if I have kept my bread to myself, not sharing it with the fatherless — but from my youth I reared him as would a father, and from my birth I guided the widow — if I have seen anyone perishing for lack of clothing, or a needy man without a garment, and his heart did not bless me for warming him with the fleece from my sheep, if I have raised my hand against the fatherless, knowing that I had influence in court, then let my arm fall from the shoulder, let it be broken off at the joint. For I dreaded destruction from God, and for fear of his splendor I could not do such things.

If I have put my trust in gold or said to pure gold, 'You are my security,' if I have rejoiced over my great wealth, the fortune my hands had gained, if I have regarded the sun in its radiance or the moon moving in splendor, so that my heart was secretly enticed and my hand offered them a kiss of homage, then these also would be sins to be judged, for I would have been unfaithful to God on high. If I have rejoiced at my enemy's misfortune or gloated over the trouble that came to him — I have not allowed my mouth to sin by invoking a curse against his life — if the men of my household have never said, 'Who has not had his fill of Job's meat?' — But no stranger had to spend the night in the street, for my door was always open to the traveler — if I have concealed my sin as men do, by hiding my guilt in my heart because I so feared the crowd and so dreaded the contempt of the clans that I kept silent and would not go outside.

Oh, that I had someone to hear me! I sign now my defense — let the Almighty answer me; let my accuser put his indictment in writing. Surely I would wear it on my shoulder, I would put it on like a crown. I would give him an account of my every step; like a prince I would approach him. — If my land cries out against me and all its furrows are wet with tears, if I have devoured its yield without payment or broken the spirit of its tenants, then let briers come up instead of wheat and weeds instead of barley. The words of Job are ended.

Job 31:1-40

O LORD my God, if I have done this and there is guilt on my hands —
if I have done evil to him who is at peace with me or without cause have
robbed my foe — then let my enemy pursue and overtake me; let him
trample my life to the ground and make me sleep in the dust. Selah.

Psalm 7:3-5

Let the LORD judge the peoples. Judge me, O LORD, according to my
righteousness, according to my integrity, O Most High.

Psalm 7:8

LORD, who may dwell in your sanctuary? Who may live on your holy hill?
He whose walk is blameless and who does what is righteous, who speaks
the truth from his heart and has no slander on his tongue, who does his
neighbor no wrong and casts no slur on his fellowman, who despises a
vile man but honors those who fear the LORD, who keeps his oath even
when it hurts, who lends his money without usury and does not accept
a bribe against the innocent. He who does these things will never be
shaken.

Psalm 15:1-5

Though you probe my heart and examine me at night, though you test
me, you will find nothing; I have resolved that my mouth will not sin.

Psalm 17:3

The LORD has dealt with me according to my righteousness; according
to the cleanness of my hands he has rewarded me.

Psalm 18:20

Who may ascend the hill of the LORD? Who may stand in his holy place?
He who has clean hands and a pure heart, who does not lift up his soul
to an idol or swear by what is false. He will receive blessing from the
LORD and vindication from God his Savior.

Psalm 24:3-5

Vindicate me, O LORD, for I have led a blameless life; I have trusted in
the LORD without wavering. Test me, O LORD, and try me, examine my
heart and my mind; for your love is ever before me, and I walk continually in your truth.

Psalm 26:1-3

The steps of a good man are ordered by the LORD, and He delights in his way. Though he fall, he shall not be utterly cast down; for the LORD upholds him with His hand. I have been young, and now am old; yet I have not seen the righteous forsaken, nor his descendants begging bread. He is ever merciful, and lends; and his descendants are blessed. Depart from evil, and do good; and dwell forevermore. For the LORD loves justice, and does not forsake His saints; they are preserved forever, but the descendants of the wicked shall be cut off. The righteous shall inherit the land, and dwell in it forever.

Psalm 37:23-29 (NKJ)

But as for me, my feet had almost slipped; I had nearly lost my foothold. For I envied the arrogant when I saw the prosperity of the wicked. They have no struggles; their bodies are healthy and strong. They are free from the burdens common to man; they are not plagued by human ills. Therefore pride is their necklace; they clothe themselves with violence. From their callous hearts comes iniquity; the evil conceits of their minds know no limits. They scoff, and speak with malice; in their arrogance they threaten oppression. Their mouths lay claim to heaven, and their tongues take possession of the earth. Therefore their people turn to them and drink up waters in abundance. They say, How can God know? Does the Most High have knowledge? This is what the wicked are like — always carefree, they increase in wealth. Surely in vain have I kept my heart pure; in vain have I washed my hands in innocence. All day long I have been plagued; I have been punished every morning. If I had said, I will speak thus, I would have betrayed your children. When I tried to understand all this, it was oppressive to me till I entered the sanctuary of God; then I understood their final destiny. Surely you place them on slippery ground; you cast them down to ruin. How suddenly are they destroyed, completely swept away by terrors!

Psalm 73:2-19

I have done what is righteous and just; do not leave me to my oppressors.

Psalm 119:121

For acquiring a disciplined and prudent life, doing what is right and just and fair.

Proverbs 1:3

Then you will understand what is right and just and fair — every good path.

Proverbs 2:9

Let love and faithfulness never leave you; bind them around your neck, write them on the tablet of your heart. Then you will win favor and a good name in the sight of God and man.

Proverbs 3:3-4

Do not say to your neighbor, "Come back later; I'll give it tomorrow" — when you now have it with you.

Proverbs 3:28

Do not plot harm against your neighbor, who lives trustfully near you.

Proverbs 3:29

Do not accuse a man for no reason — when he has done you no harm.

Proverbs 3:30

Do not envy a violent man or choose any of his ways.

Proverbs 3:31

For the LORD detests a perverse man but takes the upright into his confidence.

Proverbs 3:32

Let your eyes look straight ahead, fix your gaze directly before you. Make level paths for your feet and take only ways that are firm. Do not swerve to the right or the left; keep your foot from evil.

Proverbs 4:25-27

The man of integrity walks securely, but he who takes crooked paths will be found out.

Proverbs 10:9

The integrity of the upright guides them, but the unfaithful are destroyed by their duplicity.

Proverbs 11:3

The righteousness of the blameless makes a straight way for them, but the wicked are brought down by their own wickedness.

Proverbs 11:5

The LORD detests lying lips, but he delights in men who are truthful.

Proverbs 12:22

Righteousness guards the man of integrity, but wickedness overthrows the sinner.

Proverbs 13:6

Fools mock at making amends for sin, but goodwill is found among the upright.

Proverbs 14:9

A heart at peace gives life to the body, but envy rots the bones.

Proverbs 14:30

Folly delights a man who lacks judgment, but a man of understanding keeps a straight course.

Proverbs 15:21

Honest scales and balances are from the LORD; all the weights in the bag are of his making.

Proverbs 16:11

Better a poor man whose walk is blameless than a fool whose lips are perverse.

Proverbs 19:1

The righteous man leads a blameless life; blessed are his children after him.

Proverbs 20:7

Differing weights and differing measures — the LORD detests them both. Even a child is known by his actions, by whether his conduct is pure and right.

Proverbs 20:10-11

The LORD detests differing weights, and dishonest scales do not please him.

Proverbs 20:23

To do what is right and just is more acceptable to the LORD than sacrifice.

Proverbs 21:3

When justice is done, it brings joy to the righteous but terror to evildoers.

Proverbs 21:15

He who loves a pure heart and whose speech is gracious will have the king for his friend.

Proverbs 22:11

If you argue your case with a neighbor, do not betray another man's confidence, or he who hears it may shame you and you will never lose your bad reputation.

Proverbs 25:9-10

Like a muddied spring or a polluted well is a righteous man who gives way to the wicked.

Proverbs 25:26

Better a poor man whose walk is blameless than a rich man whose ways are perverse.

Proverbs 28:6

He who leads the upright along an evil path will fall into his own trap, but the blameless will receive a good inheritance.

Proverbs 28:10

A faithful man will be richly blessed, but one eager to get rich will not go unpunished.

Proverbs 28:20

The path of the righteous is level; O upright One, you make the way of the righteous smooth.

Isaiah 26:7

He who walks righteously and speaks what is right, who rejects gain from extortion and keeps his hand from accepting bribes, who stops his ears against plots of murder and shuts his eyes against contemplating evil — this is the man who will dwell on the heights, whose refuge will be the mountain fortress. His bread will be supplied, and water will not fail him.

Isaiah 33:15-16

This is what the LORD says: "Maintain justice and do what is right, for my salvation is close at hand and my righteousness will soon be revealed."

Isaiah 56:1

If you really change your ways and your actions and deal with each other justly, then I will let you live in this place, in the land I gave your forefathers forever and ever.

Jeremiah 7:5,7

Suppose there is a righteous man who does what is just and right. He does not oppress anyone, but returns what he took in pledge for a loan. He does not commit robbery but gives his food to the hungry and provides clothing for the naked. He does not lend at usury or take excessive interest. He withholds his hand from doing wrong and judges fairly between man and man. He follows my decrees and faithfully keeps my laws. That man is righteous; he will surely live, declares the Sovereign LORD.

Ezekiel 18:5,7-9

He has showed you, O man, what is good. And what does the LORD require of you? To act justly and to love mercy and to walk humbly with your God.

Micah 6:8

"This is what the LORD Almighty says: 'Administer true justice; show mercy and compassion to one another.'"

Zechariah 7:9

True instruction was in his mouth and nothing false was found on his lips. He walked with me in peace and uprightness, and turned many from sin.

Malachi 2:6

"Don't collect any more than you are required to," he told them. Then some soldiers asked him, "And what should we do?" He replied, "Don't extort money and don't accuse people falsely — be content with your pay."

Luke 3:13-14

Do to others as you would have them do to you.

Luke 6:31

Woe to you Pharisees, because you give God a tenth of your mint, rue and all other kinds of garden herbs, but you neglect justice and the love of God. You should have practiced the latter without leaving the former undone.

Luke 11:42

Whoever can be trusted with very little can also be trusted with much, and whoever is dishonest with very little will also be dishonest with much.

Luke 16:10

Paul looked straight at the Sanhedrin and said, "My brothers, I have fulfilled my duty to God in all good conscience to this day."

Acts 23:1

So I strive always to keep my conscience clear before God and man.

Acts 24:16

I speak the truth in Christ — I am not lying, my conscience confirms it in the Holy Spirit.

Romans 9:1

Therefore, it is necessary to submit to the authorities, not only because of possible punishment but also because of conscience.

Romans 13:5

Rather, we have renounced secret and shameful ways; we do not use deception, nor do we distort the word of God. On the contrary, by setting forth the truth plainly we commend ourselves to every man's conscience in the sight of God.

2 Corinthians 4:2

Since, then, we know what it is to fear the Lord, we try to persuade men. What we are is plain to God, and I hope it is also plain to your conscience.

2 Corinthians 5:11

Make room for us in your hearts. We have wronged no one, we have corrupted no one, we have exploited no one.

2 Corinthians 7:2

For we are taking pains to do what is right, not only in the eyes of the Lord but also in the eyes of men.

2 Corinthians 8:21

Finally, brothers, whatever is true, whatever is noble, whatever is right, whatever is pure, whatever is lovely, whatever is admirable — if anything is excellent or praiseworthy — think about such things.

Philippians 4:8

Do not lie to each other, since you have taken off your old self with its practices and have put on the new self, which is being renewed in knowledge in the image of its Creator.

Colossians 3:9-10

Servants (employees), obey your earthly masters (employers) in everything; and do it, not only when their eye is on you and to win their favor, but with sincerity of heart and reverence for the Lord. Whatever you do, work at it with all your heart, as working for the Lord, not for men.

Colossians 3:22-23

Obey them not only to win their favor when their eye is on you, but like slaves (employees) of Christ, doing the will of God from your heart.

Ephesians 6:6

On the contrary, we speak as men approved by God to be entrusted with the gospel. We are not trying to please men but God, who tests our hearts.

1 Thessalonians 2:4

The goal of this command is love, which comes from a pure heart and a good conscience and a sincere faith.

1 Timothy 1:5

They must keep hold of the deep truths of the faith with a clear conscience.

1 Timothy 3:9

Since an overseer is entrusted with God's work, he must be blameless — not overbearing, not quick-tempered, not given to drunkenness, not violent, not pursuing dishonest gain. Rather he must be hospitable, one who loves what is good, who is self-controlled, upright, holy and disciplined.

Titus 1:7-8

Pray for us. We are sure that we have a clear conscience and desire to live honorably in every way.

Hebrews 13:18

Live such good lives among the pagans that, though they accuse you of doing wrong, they may see your good deeds and glorify God on the day he visits us.

1 Peter 2:12

Keeping a clear conscience, so that those who speak maliciously against your good behavior in Christ may be ashamed of their slander.

1 Peter 3:16

Dear children, do not let anyone lead you astray. He who does what is right is righteous, just as he is righteous. He who does what is sinful is of the devil, because the devil has been sinning from the beginning. The reason the Son of God appeared was to destroy the devil's work.

1 John 3:7-8

Honesty @ Work

Do not steal. Do not lie. Do not deceive one another.

Leviticus 19:11

Do not use dishonest standards when measuring length, weight or quantity. Use honest scales and honest weights, an honest ephah and an honest hin. I am the LORD your God, who brought you out of Egypt.

Leviticus 19:35-36

Do not have two differing weights in your bag — one heavy, one light. Do not have two differing measures in your house — one large, one small. You must have accurate and honest weights and measures, so that you may live long in the land the LORD your God is giving you. For the LORD your God detests anyone who does these things, anyone who deals dishonestly.

Deuteronomy 25:13-16

When a man makes a vow to the LORD or takes an oath to obligate himself by a pledge, he must not break his word but must do everything he said.

Numbers 30:2

He who has clean hands and a pure heart, who does not lift up his soul to an idol or swear by what is false. He will receive blessing from the

You destroy those who tell lies; bloodthirsty and deceitful men the LORD abhors.

Psalm 5:6

LORD and vindication from God his Savior.

Psalm 24:4-5

There are six things the LORD hates, seven that are detestable to him: haughty eyes, a lying tongue, hands that shed innocent blood, a heart that devises wicked schemes, feet that are quick to rush into evil, a false witness who pours out lies and a man who stirs up dissension among brothers.

Proverbs 6:16-19

The tongue of the righteous is choice silver, but the heart of the wicked is of little value.

Proverbs 10:20

The LORD abhors dishonest scales, but accurate weights are his delight.

Proverbs 11:1

A truthful witness gives honest testimony, but a false witness tells lies.

Proverbs 12:17

Truthful lips endure forever, but a lying tongue lasts only a moment.

Proverbs 12:19

The LORD detests lying lips, but he delights in men who are truthful.

Proverbs 12:22

A truthful witness does not deceive, but a false witness pours out lies.

Proverbs 14:5

A truthful witness saves lives, but a false witness is deceitful.

Proverbs 14:25

Honest scales and balances are from the LORD; all the weights in the bag are of his making.

Proverbs 16:11

A false witness will not go unpunished, and he who pours out lies will not go free.

Proverbs 19:5

A false witness will not go unpunished, and he who pours out lies will perish.

Proverbs 19:9

Differing weights and differing measures — the LORD detests them both.

Proverbs 20:10

Food gained by fraud tastes sweet to a man, but he ends up with a mouth full of gravel.

Proverbs 20:17

The LORD detests differing weights, and dishonest scales do not please him.

Proverbs 20:23

An honest answer is like a kiss on the lips.

Proverbs 24:26

Do not testify against your neighbor without cause, or use your lips to deceive.

Proverbs 24:28

The righteous detest the dishonest; the wicked detest the upright.

Proverbs 29:27

He who walks righteously and speaks what is right, who rejects gain from extortion and keeps his hand from accepting bribes, who stops his ears against plots of murder and shuts his eyes against contemplating evil — his is the man who will dwell on the heights, whose refuge will be the mountain fortress. His bread will be supplied, and water will not fail him.

Isaiah 33:15-16

He has showed you, O man, what is good. And what does the LORD require of you? To act justly and to love mercy and to walk humbly with your God.

Micah 6:8

These are the things you are to do: "Speak the truth to each other, and render true and sound judgment in your courts; do not plot evil against your neighbor, and do not love to swear falsely. I hate all this," declares the LORD.

Zechariah 8:16-17

You know the commandments: Do not murder, do not commit adultery, do not steal, do not give false testimony, do not defraud, honor your father and mother.

Mark 10:19

Tax collectors also came to be baptized. "Teacher," they asked, "what should we do?" "Don't collect any more than you are required to," he told them.

Luke 3:12-13

You belong to your father, the devil, and you want to carry out your father's desire. He was a murderer from the beginning, not holding to the truth, for there is no truth in him. When he lies, he speaks his native language, for he is a liar and the father of lies.

John 8:44

Do not repay anyone evil for evil. Be careful to do what is right in the eyes of everybody.

Romans 12:17

Rather, we have renounced secret and shameful ways; we do not use deception, nor do we distort the word of God. On the contrary, by setting forth the truth plainly we commend ourselves to every man's conscience in the sight of God.

2 Corinthians 4:2

Therefore each of you must put off falsehood and speak truthfully to his neighbor, for we are all members of one body.

Ephesians 4:25

Do not lie to each other, since you have taken off your old self with its practices and have put on the new self, which is being renewed in knowledge in the image of its Creator.

Colossians 3:9-10

Live such good lives among the pagans that, though they accuse you of doing wrong, they may see your good deeds and glorify God on the day he visits us.

1 Peter 2:12

But the cowardly, the unbelieving, the vile, the murderers, the sexually immoral, those who practice magic arts, the idolaters and all liars — their place will be in the fiery lake of burning sulfur. This is the second death.

Revelation 21:8

Righteousness @ Work

Godly Character @ Work

LORD, who may dwell in your sanctuary? Who may live on your holy hill? He whose walk is blameless and who does what is righteous, who speaks the truth from his heart and has no slander on his tongue, who does his neighbor no wrong and casts no slur on his fellowman, who despises a vile man but honors those who fear the LORD, who keeps his oath even when it hurts, who lends his money without usury and does not accept a bribe against the innocent. He who does these things will never be shaken.

Psalm 15:1-5

Who may ascend the hill of the LORD? Who may stand in his holy place? He who has clean hands and a pure heart, who does not lift up his soul to an idol or swear by what is false. He will receive blessing from the LORD and vindication from God his Savior.

Psalm 24:3-5

The eyes of the LORD are on the righteous and his ears are attentive to their cry; the face of the LORD is against those who do evil, to cut off the memory of them from the earth. The righteous cry out, and the LORD hears them; he delivers them from all their troubles.

Psalm 34:15-17

A righteous man may have many troubles, but the LORD delivers him from them all; he protects all his bones, not one of them will be broken.

Psalm 34:19-20

Consider the blameless, observe the upright; there is a future for the man of peace.

Psalm 37:37

I will sing of your love and justice; to you, O LORD, I will sing praise. I will be careful to lead a blameless life — when will you come to me? I will walk in my house with blameless heart. I will set before my eyes no vile thing. The deeds of faithless men I hate; they will not cling to me. Men of perverse heart shall be far from me; I will have nothing to do with evil. Whoever slanders his neighbor in secret, him will I put to silence; whoever has haughty eyes and a proud heart, him will I not endure. My eyes will be on the faithful in the land, that they may dwell with me; he whose walk is blameless will minister to me. No one who practices deceit will dwell in my house; no one who speaks falsely will stand in my presence. Every morning I will put to silence all the wicked in the land; I will cut off every evildoer from the city of the LORD.

Psalm 101:1-8

Blessed are they who maintain justice, who constantly do what is right.

Psalm 106:3

Praise the LORD. Blessed is the man who fears the LORD, who finds great delight in his commands. His children will be mighty in the land; the generation of the upright will be blessed. Wealth and riches are in his house, and his righteousness endures forever. Even in darkness light dawns for the upright, for the gracious and compassionate and righteous man. Good will come to him who is generous and lends freely, who conducts his affairs with justice. Surely he will never be shaken; a righteous man will be remembered forever. He will have no fear of bad news; his heart is steadfast, trusting in the LORD. His heart is secure, he will have no fear; in the end he will look in triumph on his foes. He has scattered abroad his gifts to the poor, his righteousness endures forever; his horn will be lifted high in honor. The wicked man will see and be vexed, he will gnash his teeth and waste away; the longings of the wicked will come to nothing.

Psalm 112:1-10

My son, if you accept my words and store up my commands within you, turning your ear to wisdom and applying your heart to understanding, and if you call out for insight and cry aloud for understanding, and if you look for it as for silver and search for it as for hidden treasure, then you will understand the fear of the LORD and find the knowledge of God. For the LORD gives wisdom, and from his mouth come knowledge and understanding. He holds victory in store for the upright, he is a shield to those whose walk is blameless, for he guards the course of the just and protects the way of his faithful ones. Then you will understand what is right and just and fair — every good path. For wisdom will enter your heart, and knowledge will be pleasant to your soul.

Discretion will protect you, and understanding will guard you. Wisdom will save you from the ways of wicked men, from men whose words are perverse, who leave the straight paths to walk in dark ways, who delight in doing wrong and rejoice in the perverseness of evil, whose paths are crooked and who are devious in their ways. It will save you also from the adulteress, from the wayward wife with her seductive words, who has left the partner of her youth and ignored the covenant she made before God. For her house leads down to death and her paths to the spirits of the dead. None who go to her return or attain the paths of life. Thus you will walk in the ways of good men and keep to the paths of the righteous. For the upright will live in the land, and the blameless will remain in it; but the wicked will be cut off from the land, and the unfaithful will be torn from it.

Proverbs 2:1-22

Ill-gotten treasures are of no value, but righteousness delivers from death.

Proverbs 10:2

The LORD does not let the righteous go hungry but he thwarts the craving of the wicked.

Proverbs 10:3

The wages of the righteous bring them life, but the income of the wicked brings them punishment.

Proverbs 10:16

The tongue of the righteous is choice silver, but the heart of the wicked is of little value.

Proverbs 10:20

What the wicked dreads will overtake him; what the righteous desire will be granted.

Proverbs 10:24

When the storm has swept by, the wicked are gone, but the righteous stand firm forever.

Proverbs 10:25

The prospect of the righteous is joy, but the hopes of the wicked come to nothing.

Proverbs 10:28

The way of the LORD is a refuge for the righteous, but it is the ruin of those who do evil.

Proverbs 10:29

The righteous will never be uprooted, but the wicked will not remain in the land.

Proverbs 10:30

The mouth of the righteous brings forth wisdom, but a perverse tongue will be cut out.

Proverbs 10:31

The lips of the righteous know what is fitting, but the mouth of the wicked only what is perverse.

Proverbs 10:32

The integrity of the upright guides them, but the unfaithful are destroyed by their duplicity. Wealth is worthless in the day of wrath, but righteousness delivers from death. The righteousness of the blameless makes a straight way for them, but the wicked are brought down by their own wickedness. The righteousness of the upright delivers them, but the unfaithful are trapped by evil desires.

Proverbs 11:3-6

The righteous man is rescued from trouble, and it comes on the wicked instead. With his mouth the godless destroys his neighbor, but through knowledge the righteous escape. When the righteous prosper, the city rejoices; when the wicked perish, there are shouts of joy.

Proverbs 11:8-10

The wicked man earns deceptive wages, but he who sows righteousness reaps a sure reward.

Proverbs 11:18

The LORD detests men of perverse heart but he delights in those whose ways are blameless.

Proverbs 11:20

Be sure of this: The wicked will not go unpunished, but those who are righteous will go free.

Proverbs 11:21

The desire of the righteous ends only in good, but the hope of the wicked only in wrath.

Proverbs 11:23

Whoever trusts in his riches will fall, but the righteous will thrive like a green leaf.

Proverbs 11:28

The fruit of the righteous is a tree of life, and he who wins souls is wise. If the righteous receive their due on earth, how much more the ungodly and the sinner!

Proverbs 11:30-31

Wicked men are overthrown and are no more, but the house of the righteous stands firm.

Proverbs 12:7

A righteous man cares for the needs of his animal, but the kindest acts of the wicked are cruel.

Proverbs 12:10

The wicked desire the plunder of evil men, but the root of the righteous flourishes.

Proverbs 12:12

No harm befalls the righteous, but the wicked have their fill of trouble.

Proverbs 12:21

A righteous man is cautious in friendship, but the way of the wicked leads them astray.

Proverbs 12:26

In the way of righteousness there is life; along that path is immortality.

Proverbs 12:28

Righteousness guards the man of integrity, but wickedness overthrows the sinner.

Proverbs 13:6

The light of the righteous shines brightly, but the lamp of the wicked is snuffed out.

Proverbs 13:9

The righteous eat to their hearts' content, but the stomach of the wicked goes hungry.

Proverbs 13:25

Righteousness exalts a nation, but sin is a disgrace to any people.

Proverbs 14:34

The house of the righteous contains great treasure, but the income of the wicked brings them trouble.

Proverbs 15:6

The LORD detests the way of the wicked but he loves those who pursue righteousness.

Proverbs 15:9

Better a little with righteousness than much gain with injustice.

Proverbs 16:8

The righteous man leads a blameless life; blessed are his children after him.

Proverbs 20:7

To do what is right and just is more acceptable to the LORD than sacrifice.

Proverbs 21:3

He who pursues righteousness and love finds life, prosperity and honor.

Proverbs 21:21

For though a righteous man falls seven times, he rises again, but the wicked are brought down by calamity.

Proverbs 24:16

The wicked man flees though no one pursues, but the righteous are as bold as a lion.

Proverbs 28:1

An evil man is snared by his own sin, but a righteous one can sing and be glad.

Proverbs 29:6

The righteous care about justice for the poor, but the wicked have no such concern.

Proverbs 29:7

The righteous detest the dishonest; the wicked detest the upright.

Proverbs 29:27

He who walks righteously and speaks what is right, who rejects gain from extortion and keeps his hand from accepting bribes, who stops his ears against plots of murder and shuts his eyes against contemplating evil — this is the man who will dwell on the heights, whose refuge will be the mountain fortress. His bread will be supplied, and water will not fail him.

Isaiah 33:15-16

"Suppose there is a righteous man who does what is just and right. He does not eat at the mountain shrines or look to the idols of the house of Israel. He does not defile his neighbor's wife or lie with a woman during her period. He does not oppress anyone, but returns what he took in pledge for a loan. He does not commit robbery but gives his food to the hungry and provides clothing for the naked. He does not lend at usury or take excessive interest. He withholds his hand from doing wrong and judges fairly between man and man. He follows my decrees and faithfully keeps my laws. That man is righteous; he will surely live," declares the Sovereign LORD.

Ezekiel 18:5-9

For the kingdom of God is not a matter of eating and drinking, but of righteousness, peace and joy in the Holy Spirit.

Romans 14:17

We are therefore Christ's ambassadors, as though God were making his appeal through us. We implore you on Christ's behalf: Be reconciled to God. God made him who had no sin to be sin for us, so that in him we might become the righteousness of God.

2 Corinthians 5:20-21

Flee the evil desires of youth, and pursue righteousness, faith, love and peace, along with those who call on the Lord out of a pure heart.

2 Timothy 2:22

Wickedness @ Work

Godly Character @ Work

Not so the wicked! They are like chaff that the wind blows away. There-fore, the wicked will not stand in the judgment, nor sinners in the as-sembly of the righteous. For the LORD watches over the way of the righteous, but the way of the wicked will perish.

Psalm 1:4-6

The arrogant cannot stand in your presence; you hate all who do wrong. You destroy those who tell lies; bloodthirsty and deceitful men the LORD abhors.

Psalm 5:5-6

Do not drag me away with the wicked, with those who do evil, who speak cordially with their neighbors but harbor malice in their hearts. Repay them for their deeds and for their evil work; repay them for what their hands have done and bring back upon them what they deserve. Since they show no regard for the works of the LORD and what his hands have done, he will tear them down and never build them up again.

Psalm 28:3-5

The face of the LORD is against those who do evil, to cut off the memory of them from the earth.

Psalm 34:16

Do not fret because of evil men or be envious of those who do wrong; for like the grass they will soon wither, like green plants they will soon die away.

Psalm 37:1-2

For evil men will be cut off, but those who hope in the LORD will inherit the land. A little while, and the wicked will be no more; though you look for them, they will not be found.

Psalm 37:9-10

But the Lord laughs at the wicked, for he knows their day is coming. The wicked draw the sword and bend the bow to bring down the poor and needy, to slay those whose ways are upright. But their swords will pierce their own hearts, and their bows will be broken. Better the little that the righteous have than the wealth of many wicked; for the power of the wicked will be broken, but the LORD upholds the righteous.

Psalm 37:13-17

Wait for the LORD and keep his way. He will exalt you to inherit the land; when the wicked are cut off, you will see it. I have seen a wicked and ruthless man flourishing like a green tree in its native soil, but he soon passed away and was no more; though I looked for him, he could not be found.

Psalm 37:34-36

But all sinners will be destroyed; the future of the wicked will be cut off.

Psalm 37:38

But you, O God, will bring down the wicked into the pit of corruption; bloodthirsty and deceitful men will not live out half their days. But as for me, I trust in you.

Psalm 55:23

Surely God is good to Israel, to those who are pure in heart. But as for me, my feet had almost slipped; I had nearly lost my foothold. For I envied the arrogant when I saw the prosperity of the wicked. They have no struggles; their bodies are healthy and strong. They are free from the burdens common to man; they are not plagued by human ills. Therefore pride is their necklace; they clothe themselves with violence. From their callous hearts comes iniquity; the evil conceits of their minds know no limits. They scoff, and speak with malice; in their arrogance they threaten oppression. Their mouths lay claim to heaven, and their tongues take possession of the earth. Therefore their people turn to them and drink up waters in abundance. They say, How can God know? Does the Most High have knowledge? This is what the wicked are like — always care-free, they increase in wealth. Surely in vain have I kept my heart pure; in vain have I washed my hands in innocence. All day long I have been plagued; I have been punished every morning. If I had said, I will speak thus, I would have betrayed your children. When I tried to understand all this, it was oppressive to me till I entered the sanctuary of God; then I understood their final destiny. Surely you place them on slippery ground; you cast them down to ruin. How suddenly are they destroyed, com-pletely swept away by terrors!

Psalm 73:1-19

That though the wicked spring up like grass and all evildoers flourish, they will be forever destroyed.

Psalm 92:7

The LORD watches over all who love him, but all the wicked he will destroy.

Psalm 145:20

The LORD watches over the alien and sustains the fatherless and the widow, but he frustrates the ways of the wicked.

Psalm 146:9

The LORD sustains the humble but casts the wicked to the ground.

Psalm 147:6

But the wicked will be cut off from the land, and the unfaithful will be torn from it.

Proverbs 2:22

The LORD's curse is on the house of the wicked, but he blesses the home of the righteous.

Proverbs 3:33

To fear the LORD is to hate evil; I hate pride and arrogance, evil behavior and perverse speech.

Proverbs 8:13

The LORD does not let the righteous go hungry but he thwarts the craving of the wicked.

Proverbs 10:3

Blessings crown the head of the righteous, but violence overwhelms the mouth of the wicked.

Proverbs 10:6

The memory of the righteous will be a blessing, but the name of the wicked will rot.

Proverbs 10:7

The mouth of the righteous is a fountain of life, but violence overwhelms the mouth of the wicked.

Proverbs 10:11

What the wicked dreads will overtake him; what the righteous desire will be granted.

Proverbs 10:24

When the storm has swept by, the wicked are gone, but the righteous stand firm forever.

Proverbs 10:25

The fear of the LORD adds length to life, but the years of the wicked are cut short.

Proverbs 10:27

The prospect of the righteous is joy, but the hopes of the wicked come to nothing.

Proverbs 10:28

The way of the LORD is a refuge for the righteous, but it is the ruin of those who do evil.

Proverbs 10:29

The righteous will never be uprooted, but the wicked will not remain in the land.

Proverbs 10:30

The righteousness of the blameless makes a straight way for them, but the wicked are brought down by their own wickedness.

Proverbs 11:5

When a wicked man dies, his hope perishes; all he expected from his power comes to nothing.

Proverbs 11:7

The righteous man is rescued from trouble, and it comes on the wicked instead.

Proverbs 11:8

The truly righteous man attains life, but he who pursues evil goes to his death.

Proverbs 11:19

Be sure of this: The wicked will not go unpunished, but those who are righteous will go free.

Proverbs 11:21

The desire of the righteous ends only in good, but the hope of the wicked only in wrath.

Proverbs 11:23

If the righteous receive their due on earth, how much more the ungodly and the sinner!

Proverbs 11:31

A man cannot be established through wickedness, but the righteous cannot be uprooted.

Proverbs 12:3

Wicked men are overthrown and are no more, but the house of the righteous stands firm.

Proverbs 12:7

The wicked desire the plunder of evil men, but the root of the righteous flourishes.

Proverbs 12:12

The righteous hate what is false, but the wicked bring shame and disgrace.

Proverbs 13:5

Righteousness guards the man of integrity, but wickedness overthrows the sinner.

Proverbs 13:6

The light of the righteous shines brightly, but the lamp of the wicked is snuffed out.

Proverbs 13:9

A wicked messenger falls into trouble, but a trustworthy envoy brings healing.

Proverbs 13:17

Misfortune pursues the sinner, but prosperity is the reward of the righteous.

Proverbs 13:21

The righteous eat to their hearts' content, but the stomach of the wicked goes hungry.

Proverbs 13:25

He whose walk is upright fears the LORD, but he whose ways are devious despises him.

Proverbs 14:2

Evil men will bow down in the presence of the good, and the wicked at the gates of the righteous.

Proverbs 14:19

When calamity comes, the wicked are brought down, but even in death the righteous have a refuge.

Proverbs 14:32

The LORD detests the way of the wicked but he loves those who pursue righteousness.

Proverbs 15:9

The heart of the righteous weighs its answers, but the mouth of the wicked gushes evil.

Proverbs 15:28

The LORD is far from the wicked but he hears the prayer of the righteous.

Proverbs 15:29

The LORD works out everything for his own ends — even the wicked for a day of disaster.

Proverbs 16:4

An evil man is bent only on rebellion; a merciless official will be sent against him.

Proverbs 17:11

A wicked man accepts a bribe in secret to pervert the course of justice.

Proverbs 17:23

When wickedness comes, so does contempt, and with shame comes disgrace.

Proverbs 18:3

The violence of the wicked will drag them away, for they refuse to do what is right.

Proverbs 21:7

The wicked man craves evil; his neighbor gets no mercy from him.

Proverbs 21:10

The Righteous One takes note of the house of the wicked and brings the wicked to ruin.

Proverbs 21:12

When justice is done, it brings joy to the righteous but terror to evildoers.

Proverbs 21:15

A man who strays from the path of understanding comes to rest in the company of the dead.

Proverbs 21:16

A wicked man puts up a bold front, but an upright man gives thought to his ways.

Proverbs 21:29

In the paths of the wicked lie thorns and snares, but he who guards his soul stays far from them.

Proverbs 22:5

For the evil man has no future hope, and the lamp of the wicked will be snuffed out.

Proverbs 24:10

A malicious man disguises himself with his lips, but in his heart he harbors deceit. Though his speech is charming, do not believe him, for seven abominations fill his heart His malice may be concealed by deception, but his wickedness will be exposed in the assembly.

Proverbs 26:24-26

The wicked man flees though no one pursues, but the righteous are as bold as a lion.

Proverbs 28:1

Those who forsake the law praise the wicked, but those who keep the law resist them.

Proverbs 28:4

When the righteous triumph, there is great elation; but when the wicked rise to power, men go into hiding.

Proverbs 28:12

He whose walk is blameless is kept safe, but he whose ways are perverse will suddenly fall.

Proverbs 28:18

When the wicked rise to power, people go into hiding; but when the wicked perish, the righteous thrive.

Proverbs 28:28

A man who remains stiff-necked after many rebukes will suddenly be destroyed — without remedy.

Proverbs 29:1

An evil man is snared by his own sin, but a righteous one can sing and be glad.

Proverbs 29:6

When the wicked thrive, so does sin, but the righteous will see their downfall.

Proverbs 29:16

Although a wicked man commits a hundred crimes and still lives a long time, I know that it will go better with God-fearing men, who are reverent before God. Yet because the wicked do not fear God, it will not go well with them, and their days will not lengthen like a shadow.

Ecclesiastes 8:12-13

Woe to the wicked! Disaster is upon them! They will be paid back for what their hands have done.

Isaiah 3:11

There is no peace, says the LORD, for the wicked.

Isaiah 48:22

But the wicked are like the tossing sea, which cannot rest, whose waves cast up mire and mud. There is no peace, says my God, for the wicked.

Isaiah 57:20-21

God will give to each person according to what he has done. To those who by persistence in doing good seek glory, honor and immortality, he will give eternal life. But for those who are self-seeking and who reject the truth and follow evil, there will be wrath and anger. There will be trouble and distress for every human being who does evil: first for the Jew, then for the Gentile.

Romans 2:6-9

Do you not know that the wicked will not inherit the kingdom of God? Do not be deceived: Neither the sexually immoral nor idolaters nor adulterers nor male prostitutes nor homosexual offenders nor thieves nor the greedy nor drunkards nor slanderers nor swindlers will inherit the kingdom of God.

1 Corinthians 6:9-10

For we must all appear before the judgment seat of Christ, that each one may receive what is due him for the things done while in the body, whether good or bad.

2 Corinthians 5:10

The acts of the sinful nature are obvious: sexual immorality, impurity and debauchery; idolatry and witchcraft; hatred, discord, jealousy, fits of rage, selfish ambition, dissensions, factions and envy; drunkenness, orgies, and the like. I warn you, as I did before, that those who live like this will not inherit the kingdom of God.

Galatians 5:19-21

For of this you can be sure: No immoral, impure or greedy person — such a man is an idolater — has any inheritance in the kingdom of Christ and of God. Let no one deceive you with empty words, for because of such things God's wrath comes on those who are disobedient. Therefore do not be partners with them.

Ephesians 5:5-7

Justice @ Work

Do not spread false reports. Do not help a wicked man by being a malicious witness. Do not follow the crowd in doing wrong. When you give testimony in a lawsuit, do not pervert justice by siding with the crowd, and do not show favoritism to a poor man in his lawsuit.

Exodus 23:1-3

Do not deny justice to your poor people in their lawsuits. Have nothing to do with a false charge and do not put an innocent or honest person to death, for I will not acquit the guilty. Do not accept a bribe, for a bribe blinds those who see and twists the words of the righteous.

Exodus 23:6-8

Do not defraud your neighbor or rob him. Do not hold back the wages of a hired man overnight. Do not curse the deaf or put a stumbling block in front of the blind, but fear your God. I am the LORD. Do not pervert justice; do not show partiality to the poor or favoritism to the great, but judge your neighbor fairly.

Leviticus 19:13-15

When men have a dispute, they are to take it to court and the judges will decide the case, acquitting the innocent and condemning the guilty.

Deuteronomy 25:1

Do not accuse a man for no reason — when he has done you no harm.

Proverbs 3:30

A poor man's field may produce abundant food, but injustice sweeps it away.

Proverbs 13:23

Acquitting the guilty and condemning the innocent — the LORD detests them both.

Proverbs 17:15

A wicked man accepts a bribe in secret to pervert the course of justice.

Proverbs 17:23

It is not good to punish an innocent man, or to flog officials for their integrity.

Proverbs 17:26

It is not good to be partial to the wicked or to deprive the innocent of justice.

Proverbs 18:5

The first to present his case seems right, till another comes forward and questions him.

Proverbs 18:17

When justice is done, it brings joy to the righteous but terror to evildoers.

Proverbs 21:15

These also are sayings of the wise: To show partiality in judging is not good: Whoever says to the guilty, You are innocent — peoples will curse him and nations denounce him. But it will go well with those who convict the guilty, and rich blessing will come upon them.

Proverbs 24:23-25

Evil men do not understand justice, but those who seek the LORD understand it fully.

Proverbs 28:5

To show partiality is not good — yet a man will do wrong for a piece of bread.

Proverbs 28:21

By justice a king gives a country stability, but one who is greedy for bribes tears it down.

Proverbs 29:4

If a king judges the poor with fairness, his throne will always be secure.

Proverbs 29:14

Many seek an audience with a ruler, but it is from the LORD that man gets justice.

Proverbs 29:26

It is not for kings, O Lemuel — not for kings to drink wine, not for rulers to crave beer, lest they drink and forget what the law decrees, and deprive all the oppressed of their rights.

Proverbs 31:4-5

Speak up for those who cannot speak for themselves, for the rights of all who are destitute. Speak up and judge fairly; defend the rights of the poor and needy.

Proverbs 31:8-9

And I saw something else under the sun: In the place of judgment — wickedness was there, in the place of justice — wickedness was there. I thought in my heart, God will bring to judgment both the righteous and the wicked, for there will be a time for every activity, a time for every deed.

Ecclesiastes 3:16-17

If you see the poor oppressed in a district, and justice and rights denied, do not be surprised at such things; for one official is eyed by a higher one, and over them both are others higher still.

Ecclesiastes 5:8

Extortion turns a wise man into a fool, and a bribe corrupts the heart.

Ecclesiastes 7:7

Learn to do right! Seek justice, encourage the oppressed. Defend the cause of the fatherless, plead the case of the widow.

Isaiah 1:17

This is what the LORD says: "Maintain justice and do what is right, for my salvation is close at hand and my righteousness will soon be revealed."

Isaiah 56:1

To deprive a man of justice — would not the Lord see such things?

Lamentations 3:36

"These are the things you are to do: Speak the truth to each other, and render true and sound judgment in your courts; do not plot evil against your neighbor, and do not love to swear falsely. I hate all this," declares the LORD.

Zechariah 8:16-17

Settle matters quickly with your adversary who is taking you to court. Do it while you are still with him on the way, or he may hand you over to the judge, and the judge may hand you over to the officer, and you may be thrown into prison. I tell you the truth, you will not get out until you have paid the last penny.

Matthew 5:25-26

Excellence @ Work

Godly Character @ Work

God saw all that he had made, and it was very good. And there was evening, and there was morning — the sixth day.

Genesis 1:31

He is the Rock, his works are perfect, and all his ways are just. A faithful God who does no wrong, upright and just is he.

Deuteronomy 32:4

In all your ways acknowledge him, and he will make your paths straight.

Proverbs 3:6

A good name is more desirable than great riches; to be esteemed is better than silver or gold.

Proverbs 22:1

Do you see a man skilled in his work? He will serve before kings; he will not serve before obscure men.

Proverbs 22:29

Now Jeroboam was a man of standing, and when Solomon saw how well the young man did his work, he put him in charge of the whole labor force of the house of Joseph.

1 Kings 11:28

Then this Daniel distinguished himself above the governors and satraps, because an excellent spirit was in him; and the king gave thought to setting him over the whole realm.

Daniel 6:3 (NKJ)

"His master replied, 'Well done, good and faithful servant! You have been faithful with a few things; I will put you in charge of many things. Come and share your master's happiness!'"

Matthew 25:21

People were overwhelmed with amazement. "He has done everything well," they said. "He even makes the deaf hear and the mute speak."

Mark 7:37

So whether you eat or drink or whatever you do, do it all for the glory of God.

1 Corinthians 10:31

Finally, brothers, whatever is true, whatever is noble, whatever is right, whatever is pure, whatever is lovely, whatever is admirable — if anything is excellent or praiseworthy — think about such things.

Philippians 4:8

And whatever you do, whether in word or deed, do it all in the name of the Lord Jesus, giving thanks to God the Father through him.

Colossians 3:17

Whatever you do, work at it with all your heart, as working for the Lord, not for men.

Colossians 3:23

This is a trustworthy saying. And I want you to stress these things, so that those who have trusted in God may be careful to devote themselves to doing what is good. These things are excellent and profitable for everyone.

Titus 3:8

Each one should use whatever gift he has received to serve others, faithfully administering God's grace in its various forms. If anyone speaks, he should do it as one speaking the very words of God. If anyone serves, he should do it with the strength God provides, so that in all things God may be praised through Jesus Christ. To him be the glory and the power forever and ever. Amen.

1 Peter 4:10-11

His divine power has given us everything we need for life and godliness through our knowledge of him who called us by his own glory and goodness. Through these he has given us his very great and precious promises, so that through them you may participate in the divine nature and escape the corruption in the world caused by evil desires. For this very reason, make every effort to add to your faith goodness; and to goodness, knowledge; and to knowledge, self-control; and to self-control, perseverance; and to perseverance, godliness; and to godliness, brotherly kindness; and to brotherly kindness, love. For if you possess these qualities in increasing measure, they will keep you from being ineffective and unproductive in your knowledge of our Lord Jesus Christ.

2 Peter 1:3-8

Diligence @ Work

The LORD God took the man and put him in the Garden of Eden to work it and take care of it.

Genesis 2:15

Six days do your work, but on the seventh day do not work, so that your ox and your donkey may rest and the slave born in your household, and the alien as well, may be refreshed.

Exodus 23:12

Six days you shall labor and do all your work.

Deuteronomy 5:13

In everything that he undertook in the service of God's temple and in obedience to the law and the commands, he sought his God and worked wholeheartedly. And so he prospered.

2 Chronicles 31:21

Lazy hands make a man poor, but diligent hands bring wealth. He who gathers crops in summer is a wise son, but he who sleeps during harvest is a disgraceful son.

Proverbs 10:4-5

He who works his land will have abundant food, but he who chases fantasies lacks judgment.

Proverbs 12:11

Diligent hands will rule, but laziness ends in slave labor.

Proverbs 12:24

The lazy man does not roast his game, but the diligent man prizes his possessions.

Proverbs 12:27

The sluggard craves and gets nothing, but the desires of the diligent are fully satisfied.

Proverbs 13:4

Dishonest money dwindles away, but he who gathers money little by little makes it grow.

Proverbs 13:11

Where there are no oxen, the manger is empty, but from the strength of an ox comes an abundant harvest.

Proverbs 14:4

All hard work brings a profit, but mere talk leads only to poverty.

Proverbs 14:23

The laborer's appetite works for him; his hunger drives him on.

Proverbs 16:26

Do not love sleep or you will grow poor; stay awake and you will have food to spare.

Proverbs 20:13

The plans of the diligent lead to profit as surely as haste leads to poverty.

Proverbs 21:5

Do you see a man skilled in his work? He will serve before kings; he will not serve before obscure men.

Proverbs 22:29

Be sure you know the condition of your flocks, give careful attention to your herds; for riches do not endure forever, and a crown is not secure for all generations. When the hay is removed and new growth appears and the grass from the hills is gathered in, the lambs will provide you with clothing, and the goats with the price of a field. You will have plenty of goats' milk to feed you and your family and to nourish your servant girls.

Proverbs 27:23-27

He who works his land will have abundant food, but the one who chases fantasies will have his fill of poverty.

Proverbs 28:19

Ants are creatures of little strength, yet they store up their food in the summer; coneys are creatures of little power, yet they make their home in the crags; locusts have no king, yet they advance together in ranks; a lizard can be caught with the hand, yet it is found in kings' palaces.

Proverbs 30:25-28

She selects wool and flax and works with eager hands. She is like the merchant ships, bringing her food from afar. She gets up while it is still dark; she provides food for her family and portions for her servant girls. She considers a field and buys it; out of her earnings she plants a vineyard. She sets about her work vigorously; her arms are strong for her tasks. She sees that her trading is profitable, and her lamp does not go out at night. In her hand she holds the distaff and grasps the spindle with her fingers. She opens her arms to the poor and extends her hands to the needy. When it snows, she has no fear for her household; for all of them are clothed in scarlet. She makes coverings for her bed; she is clothed in fine linen and purple. Her husband is respected at the city gate, where he takes his seat among the elders of the land. She makes linen garments and sells them, and supplies the merchants with sashes. She is clothed with strength and dignity; she can laugh at the days to come. She speaks with wisdom, and faithful instruction is on her tongue.

She watches over the affairs of her household and does not eat the bread of idleness.

Proverbs 31:13-27

Whatever your hand finds to do, do it with all your might, for in the grave, where you are going, there is neither working nor planning nor knowledge nor wisdom.

Ecclessiastes 9:10

Whoever watches the wind will not plant; whoever looks at the clouds will not reap.

Ecclessiastes 11:4

Sow your seed in the morning, and at evening let not your hands be idle, for you do not know which will succeed, whether this or that, or whether both will do equally well.

Ecclesiastes 11:6

Never be lacking in zeal, but keep your spiritual fervor, serving the Lord.

Romans 12:11

He who has been stealing must steal no longer, but must work, doing something useful with his own hands, that he may have something to share with those in need.

Ephesians 4:28

Whatever you do, work at it with all your heart, as working for the Lord, not for men.

Colossians 3:23

Make it your ambition to lead a quiet life, to mind your own business and to work with your hands, just as we told you, so that your daily life may win the respect of outsiders and so that you will not be dependent on anybody.

1 Thessalonians 4:11-12

For even when we were with you, we gave you this rule: If a man will not work, he shall not eat. We hear that some among you are idle. They are not busy; they are busybodies. Such people we command and urge in the Lord Jesus Christ to settle down and earn the bread they eat.

2 Thessalonians 3:10-12

If anyone does not provide for his relatives, and especially for his immediate family, he has denied the faith and is worse than an unbeliever.

1 Timothy 5:8

Slothfulness (Laziness) @ Work

Godly Character @ Work

Go to the ant, you sluggard; consider its ways and be wise! It has no commander, no overseer or ruler, yet it stores its provisions in summer and gathers its food at harvest. How long will you lie there, you sluggard? When will you get up from your sleep? A little sleep, a little slumber, a little folding of the hands to rest — and poverty will come on you like a bandit and scarcity like an armed man.

Proverbs 6:6-11

Lazy hands make a man poor, but diligent hands bring wealth. He who gathers crops in summer is a wise son, but he who sleeps during harvest is a disgraceful son.

Proverbs 10:4-5

As vinegar to the teeth and smoke to the eyes, so is a sluggard to those who send him.

Proverbs 10:26

Diligent hands will rule, but laziness ends in slave labor.

Proverbs 12:24

The lazy man does not roast his game, but the diligent man prizes his possessions.

Proverbs 12:27

The sluggard craves and gets nothing, but the desires of the diligent are fully satisfied.

Proverbs 13:4

Good understanding wins favor, but the way of the unfaithful is hard.

Proverbs 13:15

The faithless will be fully repaid for their ways, and the good man rewarded for his.

Proverbs 14:14

All hard work brings a profit, but mere talk leads only to poverty.

Proverbs 14:23

The way of the sluggard is blocked with thorns, but the path of the upright is a highway.

Proverbs 15:19

One who is slack in his work is brother to one who destroys.

Proverbs 18:9

Laziness brings on deep sleep, and the shiftless man goes hungry.

Proverbs 19:15

The sluggard buries his hand in the dish; he will not even bring it back to his mouth!

Proverbs 19:24

A sluggard does not plow in season; so at harvest time he looks but finds nothing.

Proverbs 20:4

Do not love sleep or you will grow poor; stay awake and you will have food to spare.

Proverbs 20:13

The sluggard's craving will be the death of him, because his hands refuse to work. All day long he craves for more, but the righteous give without sparing.

Proverbs 21:25-26

The sluggard says, There is a lion outside! or, I will be murdered in the streets!

Proverbs 22:13

Listen, my son, and be wise, and keep your heart on the right path.

Proverbs 23:19

Do not join those who drink too much wine or gorge themselves on meat, for drunkards and gluttons become poor, and drowsiness clothes them in rags.

Proverbs 23:21

I went past the field of the sluggard, past the vineyard of the man who lacks judgment; thorns had come up everywhere, the ground was covered with weeds, and the stone wall was in ruins. I applied my heart to what I observed and learned a lesson from what I saw: A little sleep, a little slumber, a little folding of the hands to rest — and poverty will come on you like a bandit and scarcity like an armed man.

Proverbs 24:30-34

Like a bad tooth or a lame foot is reliance on the unfaithful in times of trouble.

Proverbs 25:19

The sluggard says, "There is a lion in the road, a fierce lion roaming the streets!" As a door turns on its hinges, so a sluggard turns on his bed. The sluggard buries his hand in the dish; he is too lazy to bring it back to his mouth. The sluggard is wiser in his own eyes than seven men who answer discreetly.

Proverbs 26:13-16

If a man is lazy, the rafters sag; if his hands are idle, the house leaks.
Ecclesiastes 10:18

"Again, it will be like a man going on a journey, who called his servants and entrusted his property to them. To one he gave five talents of money, to another two talents, and to another one talent, each according to his ability. Then he went on his journey. The man who had received the five talents went at once and put his money to work and gained five more. So also, the one with the two talents gained two more. But the man who had received the one talent went off, dug a hole in the ground and hid his master's money. "After a long time the master of those servants returned and settled accounts with them. The man who had received the five talents brought the other five. 'Master,' he said, 'you entrusted me with five talents. See, I have gained five more.' "His master replied, 'Well done, good and faithful servant! You have been faithful with a few things; I will put you in charge of many things. Come and share your master's happiness!' "The man with the two talents also came. 'Master,' he said, 'you entrusted me with two talents; see, I have gained two more.' "His master replied, 'Well done, good and faithful servant! You have been faithful with a few things; I will put you in charge of many things. Come and share your master's happiness!' "Then the man who had received the one talent came. 'Master,' he said, 'I knew that you are a hard man, harvesting where you have not sown and gathering where you have not scattered seed. So I was afraid and went out and hid your talent in the ground. See, here is what belongs to you.' "His master replied, 'You wicked, lazy servant! So you knew that I harvest where I have not sown and gather where I have not scattered seed? Well then, you should have put my money on deposit with the bankers, so that when I returned I would have received it back with interest.' "Take the talent from him and give it to the one who has the ten talents. For everyone who has will be given more, and he will have an abundance. Whoever does not have, even what he has will be taken from him. And throw that worthless servant outside, into the darkness, where there will be weeping and gnashing of teeth.'"

Matthew 25:14-30

So then, each of us will give an account of himself to God.

Romans 14:12

So whether you eat or drink or whatever you do, do it all for the glory of God.

1 Corinthians 10:31

For we must all appear before the judgment seat of Christ, that each one may receive what is due him for the things done while in the body, whether good or bad.

2 Corinthians 5:10

And whatever you do, whether in word or deed, do it all in the name of the Lord Jesus, giving thanks to God the Father through him.

Colossians 3:17

Whatever you do, work at it with all your heart, as working for the Lord, not for men.

Colossians 3:23

May the Lord direct your hearts into God's love and Christ's perseverance. In the name of the Lord Jesus Christ, we command you, brothers, to keep away from every brother who is idle and does not live according to the teaching you received from us. For you yourselves know how you ought to follow our example. We were not idle when we were with you, nor did we eat anyone's food without paying for it. On the contrary, we worked night and day, laboring and toiling so that we would not be a burden to any of you. We did this, not because we do not have the right to such help, but in order to make ourselves a model for you to follow. For even when we were with you, we gave you this rule: "If a man will not work, he shall not eat." We hear that some among you are idle. They are not busy; they are busybodies. Such people we command and urge in the Lord Jesus Christ to settle down and earn the bread they eat. And as for you, brothers, never tire of doing what is right. If anyone does not obey our instruction in this letter, take special note of him. Do not associate with him, in order that he may feel ashamed. Yet do not regard him as an enemy, but warn him as a brother.

2 Thessalonians 3:5-15

God is not unjust; he will not forget your work and the love you have shown him as you have helped his people and continue to help them. We want each of you to show this same diligence to the very end, in order to make your hope sure. We do not want you to become lazy, but to imitate those who through faith and patience inherit what has been promised.

Hebrews 6:10-12

Humility @ Work

Godly Character @ Work

If my people, who are called by my name, will humble themselves and pray and seek my face and turn from their wicked ways, then will I hear from heaven and will forgive their sin and will heal their land.

2 Chronicles 7:14

He guides the humble in what is right and teaches them his way.

Psalm 25:9

But the meek will inherit the land and enjoy great peace.

Psalm 37:11

My heart is not proud, O LORD, my eyes are not haughty; I do not concern myself with great matters or things too wonderful for me.
But I have stilled and quieted my soul; like a weaned child with its mother, like a weaned child is my soul within me.

Psalm 131:1-2

Though the LORD is on high, he looks upon the lowly, but the proud he knows from afar.

Psalm 138:6

The LORD sustains the humble but casts the wicked to the ground.

Psalm 147:6

Do not be wise in your own eyes; fear the LORD and shun evil.

Proverbs 3:7

He mocks proud mockers but gives grace to the humble.

Proverbs 3:34

The wise in heart accept commands, but a chattering fool comes to ruin.

Proverbs 10:8

When pride comes, then comes disgrace, but with humility comes wisdom.

Proverbs 11:2

Better to be a nobody and yet have a servant than pretend to be somebody and have no food.

Proverbs 12:9

The way of a fool seems right to him, but a wise man listens to advice.

Proverbs 12:15

The fear of the LORD teaches a man wisdom, and humility comes before honor.

Proverbs 15:33

Better to be lowly in spirit and among the oppressed than to share plunder with the proud.

Proverbs 16:19

Before his downfall a man's heart is proud, but humility comes before honor.

Proverbs 18:12

Humility and the fear of the LORD bring wealth and honor and life.

Proverbs 22:4

Do not exalt yourself in the king's presence, and do not claim a place among great men.

Proverbs 25:6

It is better for him to say to you, "Come up here," than for him to humiliate you before a nobleman.

Proverbs 25:7a

It is not good to eat too much honey, nor is it honorable to seek one's own honor.

Proverbs 25:27

Let another praise you, and not your own mouth; someone else, and not your own lips.

Proverbs 27:2

The crucible for silver and the furnace for gold, but man is tested by the praise he receives.

Proverbs 27:21

A man's pride brings him low, but a man of lowly spirit gains honor.

Proverbs 29:23

If you have played the fool and exalted yourself, or if you have planned evil, clap your hand over your mouth!

Proverbs 30:32

Do not be quick with your mouth, do not be hasty in your heart to utter anything before God. God is in heaven and you are on earth, so let your words be few.

Ecclesiastes 5:2

Once more the humble will rejoice in the LORD; the needy will rejoice in the Holy One of Israel.

Isaiah 29:19

"Has not my hand made all these things, and so they came into being?" declares the LORD. "This is the one I esteem: he who is humble and contrite in spirit, and trembles at my word."

Isaiah 66:2

This is what the LORD says: "Let not the wise man boast of his wisdom or the strong man boast of his strength or the rich man boast of his riches, but let him who boasts boast about this: that he understands and knows me, that I am the LORD, who exercises kindness, justice and righteousness on earth, for in these I delight," declares the LORD.

Jeremiah 9:23-24

He has showed you, O man, what is good. And what does the LORD require of you? To act justly and to love mercy and to walk humbly with your God.

Micah 6:8

Blessed are the poor in spirit, for theirs is the kingdom of heaven.

Matthew 5:3

Take my yoke upon you and learn from me, for I am gentle and humble in heart, and you will find rest for your souls.

Matthew 11:29

He called a little child and had him stand among them. And he said:
"I tell you the truth, unless you change and become like little children, you will never enter the kingdom of heaven. Therefore, whoever humbles himself like this child is the greatest in the kingdom of heaven."

Matthew 18:2-4

Not so with you. Instead, whoever wants to become great among you must be your servant, and whoever wants to be first must be your slave.

Matthew 20:26-27

For whoever exalts himself will be humbled, and whoever humbles himself will be exalted.

Matthew 23:12

They came to Capernaum. When he was in the house, he asked them, "What were you arguing about on the road?" But they kept quiet because on the way they had argued about who was the greatest. Sitting down, Jesus called the Twelve and said, "If anyone wants to be first, he must be the very last, and the servant of all." He took a little child and had him stand among them. Taking him in his arms, he said to them,

"Whoever welcomes one of these little children in my name welcomes me; and whoever welcomes me does not welcome me but the one who sent me."

Mark 9:33-37

Not so with you. Instead, whoever wants to become great among you must be your servant, and whoever wants to be first must be slave of all.

Mark 10:43-44

He has brought down rulers from their thrones but has lifted up the humble.

Luke 1:52

An argument started among the disciples as to which of them would be the greatest. Jesus, knowing their thoughts, took a little child and had him stand beside him. Then he said to them, "Whoever welcomes this little child in my name welcomes me; and whoever welcomes me welcomes the one who sent me. For he who is least among you all — he is the greatest."

Luke 9:46-48

But when you are invited, take the lowest place, so that when your host comes, he will say to you, "Friend, move up to a better place." Then you will be honored in the presence of all your fellow guests. For everyone who exalts himself will be humbled, and he who humbles himself will be exalted.

Luke 14:10-11

"But the tax collector stood at a distance. He would not even look up to heaven, but beat his breast and said, 'God, have mercy on me, a sinner.' "I tell you that this man, rather than the other, went home justified before God. For everyone who exalts himself will be humbled, and he who humbles himself will be exalted."

Luke 18:13-14

Also a dispute arose among them as to which of them was considered to be greatest. Jesus said to them, "The kings of the Gentiles lord it over them; and those who exercise authority over them call themselves Benefactors. But you are not to be like that. Instead, the greatest among you should be like the youngest, and the one who rules like the one who serves. For who is greater, the one who is at the table or the one who serves? Is it not the one who is at the table? But I am among you as one who serves."

Luke 22:24-27

For by the grace given me I say to every one of you: Do not think of yourself more highly than you ought, but rather think of yourself with sober judgment, in accordance with the measure of faith God has given you.

Romans 12:3

Be devoted to one another in brotherly love. Honor one another above yourselves.

Romans 12:10

Live in harmony with one another. Do not be proud, but be willing to associate with people of low position. Do not be conceited.

Romans 12:16

He chose the lowly things of this world and the despised things — and the things that are not — to nullify the things that are, so that no one may boast before him.

1 Corinthians 1:28-29

So, if you think you are standing firm, be careful that you don't fall!

1 Corinthians 10:12

Love is patient, love is kind. It does not envy, it does not boast, it is not proud.

1 Corinthians 13:4

Let us not become conceited, provoking and envying each other.

Galatians 5:26

May I never boast except in the cross of our Lord Jesus Christ, through which the world has been crucified to me, and I to the world.

Galatians 6:14

Be completely humble and gentle; be patient, bearing with one another in love.

Ephesians 4:2

Submit to one another out of reverence for Christ.

Ephesians 5:21

Do nothing out of selfish ambition or vain conceit, but in humility consider others better than yourselves. Each of you should look not only to your own interests, but also to the interests of others. Your attitude should be the same as that of Christ Jesus: Who, being in very nature God, did not consider equality with God something to be grasped, but made himself nothing, taking the very nature of a servant, being made in human likeness. And being found in appearance as a man, he humbled himself and became obedient to death — even death on a cross! Therefore God exalted him to the highest place and gave him the name that is above every name, that at the name of Jesus every knee should bow, in heaven and on earth and under the earth, and every tongue confess that Jesus Christ is Lord, to the glory of God the Father.

Philippians 2:3-11

Therefore, as God's chosen people, holy and dearly loved, clothe yourselves with compassion, kindness, humility, gentleness and patience.

Colossians 3:12

The brother in humble circumstances ought to take pride in his high position. But the one who is rich should take pride in his low position, because he will pass away like a wild flower.

James 1:9-10

But he gives us more grace. That is why Scripture says: "God opposes the proud but gives grace to the humble."

James 4:6

Humble yourselves before the Lord, and he will lift you up.

James 4:10

Young men, in the same way be submissive to those who are older. All of you, clothe yourselves with humility toward one another, because, God opposes the proud but gives grace to the humble. Humble yourselves, therefore, under God's mighty hand, that he may lift you up in due time.

1 Peter 5:5-6

Pride and Arrogance @ Work

I will break down your stubborn pride and make the sky above you like iron and the ground beneath you like bronze.

Leviticus 26:19

You may say to yourself, "My power and the strength of my hands have produced this wealth for me." But remember the LORD your God, for it is he who gives you the ability to produce wealth, and so confirms his covenant, which he swore to your forefathers, as it is today. If you ever forget the LORD your God and follow other gods and worship and bow down to them, I testify against you today that you will surely be destroyed.

Deuteronomy 8:17-19

Do not keep talking so proudly or let your mouth speak such arrogance, for the LORD is a God who knows, and by him deeds are weighed.

1 Samuel 2:3

Love the LORD, all his saints! The LORD preserves the faithful, but the proud he pays back in full. Be strong and take heart, all you who hope in the LORD.

Psalm 31:23-24

Why do you boast of evil, you mighty man? Why do you boast all day long, you who are a disgrace in the eyes of God? Your tongue plots destruction; it is like a sharpened razor, you who practice deceit. You love evil rather than good, falsehood rather than speaking the truth. Selah. You love every harmful word, O you deceitful tongue! Surely God will bring you down to everlasting ruin: He will snatch you up and tear you from your tent; he will uproot you from the land of the living. Selah. The righteous will see and fear; they will laugh at him, saying, "Here now is the man who did not make God his stronghold but trusted in his great wealth and grew strong by destroying others!" But I am like an olive tree flourishing in the house of God; I trust in God's unfailing love for ever and ever. I will praise you forever for what you have done; in your name I will hope, for your name is good. I will praise you in the presence of your saints.

Psalm 52:1-9

But as for me, my feet had almost slipped; I had nearly lost my foothold. For I envied the arrogant when I saw the prosperity of the wicked. They have no struggles; their bodies are healthy and strong. They are free from the burdens common to man; they are not plagued by human ills. Therefore pride is their necklace; they clothe themselves with violence. From their callous hearts comes iniquity; the evil conceits of their minds know no limits. They scoff, and speak with malice; in their arrogance they threaten oppression. Their mouths lay claim to heaven, and their tongues take possession of the earth. Therefore their people turn to them and drink up waters in abundance. They say, "How can God know? Does the Most High have knowledge?" This is what the wicked are like — always carefree, they increase in wealth. Surely in vain have I kept my heart pure; in vain have I washed my hands in innocence. All day long I have been plagued; I have been punished every morning. If I had said, "I will speak thus," I would have betrayed your children. When I tried to understand all this, it was oppressive to me till I entered the sanctuary of God; then I understood their final destiny. Surely you place them on slippery ground; you cast them down to ruin. How suddenly are they destroyed, completely swept away by terrors!

Psalm 73:2-19

Whoever slanders his neighbor in secret, him will I put to silence; whoever has haughty eyes and a proud heart, him will I not endure.

Psalm 101:5

Though the LORD is on high, he looks upon the lowly, but the proud he knows from afar.

Psalm 138:6

Do not be wise in your own eyes; fear the LORD and shun evil.

Proverbs 3:7

This will bring health to your body and nourishment to your bones.

Proverbs 3:8

The LORD's curse is on the house of the wicked, but he blesses the home of the righteous.

Proverbs 3:33

He mocks proud mockers but gives grace to the humble.

Proverbs 3:34

There are six things the LORD hates, seven that are detestable to him: haughty eyes, a lying tongue, hands that shed innocent blood, a heart that devises wicked schemes, feet that are quick to rush into evil, a false witness who pours out lies and a man who stirs up dissension among brothers.

Proverbs 6:16-19

To fear the LORD is to hate evil; I hate pride and arrogance, evil behavior and perverse speech.

Proverbs 8:13

When pride comes, then comes disgrace, but with humility comes wisdom.

Proverbs 11:2

Better to be a nobody and yet have a servant than pretend to be somebody and have no food.

Proverbs 12:9

Pride only breeds quarrels, but wisdom is found in those who take advice.

Proverbs 13:10

The LORD tears down the proud man's house but he keeps the widow's boundaries intact.

Proverbs 15:25

The LORD detests all the proud of heart. Be sure of this: They will not go unpunished.

Proverbs 16:5

Pride goes before destruction, a haughty spirit before a fall. Better to be lowly in spirit and among the oppressed than to share plunder with the proud.

Proverbs 16:18-19

Before his downfall a man's heart is proud, but humility comes before honor.

Proverbs 18:12

Haughty eyes and a proud heart, the lamp of the wicked, are sin!

Proverbs 21:4

The proud and arrogant man — Mocker is his name; he behaves with overweening pride.

Proverbs 21: 24

It is not good to eat too much honey, nor is it honorable to seek one's own honor.

Proverbs 25:27

Do you see a man wise in his own eyes? There is more hope for a fool than for him.

Proverbs 26:12

Let another praise you, and not your own mouth; someone else, and not your own lips.

Proverbs 27:2

A rich man may be wise in his own eyes, but a poor man who has discernment sees through him.

Proverbs 28:11

He who trusts in himself is a fool, but he who walks in wisdom is kept safe.

Proverbs 28:26

A man's pride brings him low, but a man of lowly spirit gains honor.

Proverbs 29:23

The eyes of the arrogant man will be humbled and the pride of men brought low; the LORD alone will be exalted in that day.

Isaiah 2:11

This is what the LORD says: "Let not the wise man boast of his wisdom or the strong man boast of his strength or the rich man boast of his riches, but let him who boasts boast about this: that he understands and knows me, that I am the LORD, who exercises kindness, justice and righteousness on earth, for in these I delight," declares the LORD.

Jeremiah 9:23-24

Hear and pay attention, do not be arrogant, for the LORD has spoken.

Jeremiah 13:15

The greatest among you will be your servant. For whoever exalts himself will be humbled, and whoever humbles himself will be exalted.

Matthew 23:11-12

For from within, out of men's hearts, come evil thoughts, sexual immorality, theft, murder, adultery, greed, malice, deceit, lewdness, envy, slander, arrogance and folly. All these evils come from inside and make a man unclean.

Mark 7:21-23

"When someone invites you to a wedding feast, do not take the place of honor, for a person more distinguished than you may have been invited.

If so, the host who invited both of you will come and say to you, 'Give this man your seat.' Then, humiliated, you will have to take the least important place. But when you are invited, take the lowest place, so that when your host comes, he will say to you, 'Friend, move up to a better place.' Then you will be honored in the presence of all your fellow guests. For everyone who exalts himself will be humbled, and he who humbles himself will be exalted.

Luke 14:8-11

For by the grace given me I say to every one of you: Do not think of yourself more highly than you ought, but rather think of yourself with sober judgment, in accordance with the measure of faith God has given you.

Romans 12:3

Live in harmony with one another. Do not be proud, but be willing to associate with people of low position. Do not be conceited.

Romans 12:16

Do not deceive yourselves. If any one of you thinks he is wise by the standards of this age, he should become a "fool" so that he may become wise. For the wisdom of this world is foolishness in God's sight. As it is written: "He catches the wise in their craftiness."

1 Corinthians 3:18-19

Love is patient, love is kind. It does not envy, it does not boast, it is not proud. It is not rude, it is not self-seeking, it is not easily angered, it keeps no record of wrongs. Love does not delight in evil but rejoices with the truth. It always protects, always trusts, always hopes, always perseveres. Love never fails.

1 Corinthians 13:4-8

But, let him who boasts boast in the Lord. For it is not the one who commends himself who is approved, but the one whom the Lord commends.

2 Corinthians 10:17-18

If anyone thinks he is something when he is nothing, he deceives himself.

Galatians 6:3

Do nothing out of selfish ambition or vain conceit, but in humility consider others better than yourselves. Each of you should look not only to your own interests, but also to the interests of others. Your attitude should be the same as that of Christ Jesus: Who, being in very nature God, did not consider equality with God something to be grasped, but made himself nothing, taking the very nature of a servant, being made in human likeness. And being found in appearance as a man, he humbled himself and became obedient to death — even death on a cross! Therefore God exalted him to the highest place and gave him the name that is above every name, that at the name of Jesus every knee should bow, in heaven and on earth and under the earth.

Philippians 2:3-10

Command those who are rich in this present world not to be arrogant nor to put their hope in wealth, which is so uncertain, but to put their hope in God, who richly provides us with everything for our enjoyment. Command them to do good, to be rich in good deeds, and to be generous and willing to share. In this way they will lay up treasure for themselves as a firm foundation for the coming age, so that they may take hold of the life that is truly life.

1 Timothy 6:17-19

But mark this: There will be terrible times in the last days. People will be lovers of themselves, lovers of money, boastful, proud, abusive, disobedient to their parents, ungrateful, unholy, without love, unforgiving, slanderous, without self-control, brutal, not lovers of the good, treacherous, rash, conceited, lovers of pleasure rather than lovers of God — having a form of godliness but denying its power. Have nothing to do with them.

2 Timothy 3:1-5

But he gives us more grace. That is why Scripture says: "God opposes the proud but gives grace to the humble."

James 4:6

Young men, in the same way be submissive to those who are older. All of you, clothe yourselves with humility toward one another, because, God opposes the proud but gives grace to the humble.

1 Peter 5:5

Do not love the world or anything in the world. If anyone loves the world, the love of the Father is not in him. For everything in the world the cravings of sinful man, the lust of his eyes and the boasting of what he has and does — comes not from the Father but from the world. The world and its desires pass away, but the man who does the will of God lives forever.

1 John 2:15-17

Envy and Jealousy @ Work

Godly Character @ Work

Resentment kills a fool, and envy slays the simple.

Job 5:2

Do not fret because of evil men or be envious of those who do wrong; for like the grass they will soon wither, like green plants they will soon die away.

Psalm 37:1-2

Be still before the LORD and wait patiently for him; do not fret when men succeed in their ways, when they carry out their wicked schemes.

Psalm 37:7

Do not be overawed when a man grows rich, when the splendor of his house increases; for he will take nothing with him when he dies, his splendor will not descend with him. Though while he lived he counted himself blessed — and men praise you when you prosper — he will join the generation of his fathers, who will never see the light. A man who has riches without understanding is like the beasts that perish.

Psalm 49:16-20

For I envied the arrogant when I saw the prosperity of the wicked. They have no struggles; their bodies are healthy and strong. They are free from the burdens common to man; they are not plagued by human ills. Therefore pride is their necklace; they clothe themselves with violence. From their callous hearts comes iniquity; the evil conceits of their minds know no limits. They scoff, and speak with malice; in their arrogance they threaten oppression. Their mouths lay claim to heaven, and their tongues take possession of the earth. Therefore their people turn to them and drink up waters in abundance. They say, "How can God know? Does the Most High have knowledge?" This is what the wicked are like — always carefree, they increase in wealth. Surely in vain have I kept my heart pure; in vain have I washed my hands in innocence. All day long I have been plagued; I have been punished every morning. If I had said, "I will speak thus," I would have betrayed your children. When I tried to understand all this, it was oppressive to me till I entered the sanctuary of God; then I understood their final destiny. Surely you place them on slippery ground; you cast them down to ruin. How suddenly are they destroyed, completely swept away by terrors!

Psalm 73:3-19

Do not envy a violent man or choose any of his ways,

Proverbs 3:31

A heart at peace gives life to the body, but envy rots the bones.

Proverbs 14:30

Do not let your heart envy sinners, but always be zealous for the fear of the LORD.

Proverbs 23:17

Do not envy wicked men, do not desire their company; for their hearts plot violence, and their lips talk about making trouble.

Proverbs 24:1-2

Do not fret because of evil men or be envious of the wicked, for the evil man has no future hope, and the lamp of the wicked will be snuffed out.

Proverbs 24:19-20

Anger is cruel and fury overwhelming, but who can stand before jealousy?

Proverbs 27:4

And I saw that all labor and all achievement spring from man's envy of his neighbor. This too is meaningless, a chasing after the wind.

Ecclesiastes 4:4

They have become filled with every kind of wickedness, evil, greed and depravity. They are full of envy, murder, strife, deceit and malice. They are gossips, slanderers, God-haters, insolent, arrogant and boastful; they invent ways of doing evil; they disobey their parents; they are senseless, faithless, heartless, ruthless. Although they know God's righteous decree that those who do such things deserve death, they not only continue to do these very things but also approve of those who practice them.

Romans 1:29-32

Let us behave decently, as in the daytime, not in orgies and drunkenness, not in sexual immorality and debauchery, not in dissension and jealousy. Rather, clothe yourselves with the Lord Jesus Christ, and do not think about how to gratify the desires of the sinful nature.

Romans 13:13-14

You are still worldly. For since there is jealousy and quarreling among you, are you not worldly? Are you not acting like mere men?

1 Corinthians 3:3

Love is patient, love is kind. It does not envy, it does not boast, it is not proud.

1 Corinthians 13:4

The acts of the sinful nature are obvious: sexual immorality, impurity and debauchery; idolatry and witchcraft; hatred, discord, jealousy, fits of rage, selfish ambition, dissensions, factions and envy; drunkenness, orgies, and the like. I warn you, as I did before, that those who live like this will not inherit the kingdom of God.

Galatians 5:19-21

Let us not become conceited, provoking and envying each other.

Galatians 5:26

At one time we too were foolish, disobedient, deceived and enslaved by all kinds of passions and pleasures. We lived in malice and envy, being hated and hating one another. But when the kindness and love of God our Savior appeared, he saved us, not because of righteous things we had done, but because of his mercy. He saved us through the washing of rebirth and renewal by the Holy Spirit.

Titus 3:3-5

But if you harbor bitter envy and selfish ambition in your hearts, do not boast about it or deny the truth. Such wisdom does not come down from heaven but is earthly, unspiritual, of the devil. For where you have envy and selfish ambition, there you find disorder and every evil practice. But the wisdom that comes from heaven is first of all pure; then peace-loving, considerate, submissive, full of mercy and good fruit, impartial and sincere.

James 3:14-17

Therefore, rid yourselves of all malice and all deceit, hypocrisy, envy, and slander of every kind.

1 Peter 2:1

Responsibility @ Work

Godly Character @ Work

Love the LORD, all his saints! The LORD preserves the faithful, but the proud he pays back in full.

Psalm 31:23

Let love and faithfulness never leave you; bind them around your neck, write them on the tablet of your heart.

Proverbs 3:3

Then you will win favor and a good name in the sight of God and man.

Proverbs 3:4

Go to the ant, you sluggard; consider its ways and be wise! It has no commander, no overseer or ruler, yet it stores its provisions in summer and gathers its food at harvest.

Proverbs 6:6-8

How long will you lie there, you sluggard? When will you get up from your sleep?

Proverbs 6:9

A little sleep, a little slumber, a little folding of the hands to rest — and poverty will come on you like a bandit and scarcity like an armed man.

Proverbs 6:10-11

A wicked messenger falls into trouble, but a trustworthy envoy brings healing.

Proverbs 13:17

One who is slack in his work is brother to one who destroys.

Proverbs 18:9

Many a man claims to have unfailing love, but a faithful man who can find?

Proverbs 20:6

Even a child is known by his actions, by whether his conduct is pure and right.

Proverbs 20:11

It is a trap for a man to dedicate something rashly and only later to consider his vows.

Proverbs 20:25

Finish your outdoor work and get your fields ready; after that, build your house.

Proverbs 24:27

He who works his land will have abundant food, but the one who chases fantasies will have his fill of poverty.

Proverbs 28:19

A faithful man will be richly blessed, but one eager to get rich will not go unpunished.

Proverbs 28:20

For by your words you will be acquitted, and by your words you will be condemned.

Matthew 12:37

"Again, it will be like a man going on a journey, who called his servants and entrusted his property to them. To one he gave five talents of money, to another two talents, and to another one talent, each according to his ability. Then he went on his journey. The man who had received the five talents went at once and put his money to work and gained five more. So also, the one with the two talents gained two more. But the man who had received the one talent went off, dug a hole in the ground and hid his master's money. "After a long time the master of those servants returned and settled accounts with them. The man who had received the five talents brought the other five. 'Master,' he said, 'you entrusted me with five talents. See, I have gained five more.' "His master replied, 'Well done, good and faithful servant! You have been faithful with a few things; I will put you in charge of many things. Come and share your master's happiness!' "The man with the two talents also came. 'Master,' he said, 'you entrusted me with two talents; see, I have gained two more.' "His master replied, 'Well done, good and faithful servant! You have been faithful with a few things; I will put you in charge of many things. Come and share your master's happiness!' "Then the man who had received the one talent came. 'Master,' he said, 'I knew that you are a hard man, harvesting where you have not sown and gathering where you have not scattered seed. So I was afraid and went out and hid your talent in the ground. See, here is what belongs to you.' "His master replied, 'You wicked, lazy servant! So you knew that I harvest where I have not sown and gather where I have not scattered seed? Well then, you should have put my money on deposit with the bankers, so that when I returned I would have received it back with interest. "'Take the talent from him and give it to the one who has the ten talents. For everyone who has will be given more, and he will have an abundance. Whoever does not have, even what he has will be taken from him.'"

Matthew 25:14-29

The Lord answered, "Who then is the faithful and wise manager, whom the master puts in charge of his servants to give them their food allowance at the proper time? It will be good for that servant whom the master finds doing so when he returns. I tell you the truth, he will put him in charge of all his possessions."

Luke 12:42-44

Whoever can be trusted with very little can also be trusted with much, and whoever is dishonest with very little will also be dishonest with much. So if you have not been trustworthy in handling worldly wealth, who will trust you with true riches? And if you have not been trustworthy with someone else's property, who will give you property of your own?

Luke 16:10-12

He said: "A man of noble birth went to a distant country to have himself appointed king and then to return. So he called ten of his servants and gave them ten minas. 'Put this money to work,' he said, 'until I come back.' But his subjects hated him and sent a delegation after him to say, 'We don't want this man to be our king.' He was made king, however, and returned home. Then he sent for the servants to whom he had given the money, in order to find out what they had gained with it. "The first one came and said, 'Sir, your mina has earned ten more.' "'Well done, my good servant!' his master replied. 'Because you have been trustworthy in a very small matter, take charge of ten cities.'

"The second came and said, 'Sir, your mina has earned five more.' His master answered, 'You take charge of five cities.' Then another servant came and said, 'Sir, here is your mina; I have kept it laid away in a piece of cloth. I was afraid of you, because you are a hard man. You take out what you did not put in and reap what you did not sow.' His master replied, 'I will judge you by your own words, you wicked servant! You knew, did you, that I am a hard man, taking out what I did not put in, and reaping what I did not sow? Why then didn't you put my money on deposit, so that when I came back, I could have collected it with interest? Then he said to those standing by, 'Take his mina away from him and give it to the one who has ten minas.' " Sir," they said, he already has ten!' He replied, 'I tell you that to everyone who has, more will be given, but as for the one who has nothing, even what he has will be taken away.'"

Luke 19:12-26

Now it is required that those who have been given a trust must prove faithful.

1 Corinthians 4:2

Respect @ Work

Honor your father and your mother, so that you may live long in the land the LORD your God is giving you.

Exodus 20:12

Rise in the presence of the aged, show respect for the elderly and revere your God. I am the LORD.

Leviticus 19:32

Do not withhold good from those who deserve it, when it is in your power to act.

Proverbs 3:27

A kindhearted woman gains respect, but ruthless men gain only wealth.

Proverbs 11:16

Do not exalt yourself in the king's presence, and do not claim a place among great men.

Proverbs 25:6

Be devoted to one another in brotherly love. Honor one another above yourselves.

Romans 12:10

Give everyone what you owe him: If you owe taxes, pay taxes; if revenue, then revenue; if respect, then respect; if honor, then honor.

Romans 13:7

Slaves (employees), obey your earthly masters (employers) with respect and fear, and with sincerity of heart, just as you would obey Christ. Obey them not only to win their favor when their eye is on you, but like slaves (employees) of Christ, doing the will of God from your heart.

Ephesians 6:5-6

Do nothing out of selfish ambition or vain conceit, but in humility consider others better than yourselves. Each of you should look not only to your own interests, but also to the interests of others.

Philippians 2:3-4

Slaves (employees), obey your earthly masters (employers) in everything; and do it, not only when their eye is on you and to win their favor, but with sincerity of heart and reverence for the Lord. Whatever you do, work at it with all your heart, as working for the Lord, not for men, since you know that you will receive an inheritance from the Lord as a reward. It is the Lord Christ you are serving. Anyone who does wrong will be repaid for his wrong, and there is no favoritism.

Colossians 3:22-25

Do not rebuke an older man harshly, but exhort him as if he were your father. Treat younger men as brothers, older women as mothers, and younger women as sisters, with absolute purity.

1 Timothy 5:1-2

All who are under the yoke of slavery should consider their masters (employers) worthy of full respect, so that God's name and our teaching may not be slandered. Those who have believing masters (employers) are not to show less respect for them because they are brothers. Instead, they are to serve them even better, because those who benefit from their service are believers, and dear to them. These are the things you are to teach and urge on them.

1 Timothy 6:1-2

Teach slaves (employees) to be subject to their masters (employers) in everything, to try to please them, not to talk back to them, and not to steal from them, but to show that they can be fully trusted, so that in every way they will make the teaching about God our Savior attractive.

Titus 2:9-10

Remind the people to be subject to rulers and authorities, to be obedient, to be ready to do whatever is good, to slander no one, to be peaceable and considerate, and to show true humility toward all men.

Titus 3:1-2

Show proper respect to everyone: Love the brotherhood of believers, fear God, honor the king. Slaves (employees), submit yourselves to your masters (employers) with all respect, not only to those who are good and considerate, but also to those who are harsh.

1 Peter 2:17-18

Honor @ Work

Godly Character @ Work

Honor your father and your mother, so that you may live long in the land the LORD your God is giving you.

Exodus 20:12

Yours, O LORD, is the greatness and the power and the glory and the majesty and the splendor, for everything in heaven and earth is yours. Yours, O LORD, is the kingdom; you are exalted as head over all. Wealth and honor come from you; you are the ruler of all things. In your hands are strength and power to exalt and give strength to all.

1 Chronicles 29:11-12

My salvation and my honor depend on God; he is my mighty rock, my refuge.

Psalm 62:7

For the LORD God is a sun and shield; the LORD bestows favor and honor; no good thing does he withhold from those whose walk is blameless.

Psalm 84:11

Blessed is the man who finds wisdom, the man who gains understanding, for she is more profitable than silver and yields better returns than

167

gold. She is more precious than rubies; nothing you desire can compare with her. Long life is in her right hand; in her left hand are riches and honor.

Proverbs 3:13-16

The wise inherit honor, but fools he holds up to shame.

Proverbs 3:35

Wisdom is supreme; therefore get wisdom. Though it cost all you have, get understanding.

Proverbs 4:7

Esteem her, and she will exalt you; embrace her, and she will honor you.

Proverbs 4:8

He who ignores discipline comes to poverty and shame, but whoever heeds correction is honored.

Proverbs 13:18

The fear of the LORD teaches a man wisdom, and humility comes before honor.

Proverbs 15:33

Before his downfall a man's heart is proud, but humility comes before honor.

Proverbs 18:12

It is to a man's honor to avoid strife, but every fool is quick to quarrel.

Proverbs 20:3

He who pursues righteousness and love finds life, prosperity and honor.

Proverbs 21:21

Humility and the fear of the LORD bring wealth and honor and life.

Proverbs 22:4

It is not good to eat too much honey, nor is it honorable to seek one's own honor.

Proverbs 25:27

Like snow in summer or rain in harvest, honor is not fitting for a fool.

Proverbs 26:1

Like tying a stone in a sling is the giving of honor to a fool.

Proverbs 26:8

A man's pride brings him low, but a man of lowly spirit gains honor.

Proverbs 29:23

As dead flies give perfume a bad smell, so a little folly outweighs wisdom and honor.

Ecclesiastes 10:1

He who speaks on his own does so to gain honor for himself, but he who works for the honor of the one who sent him is a man of truth; there is nothing false about him.

John 7:18

To those who by persistence in doing good seek glory, honor and immortality, he will give eternal life. But for those who are self-seeking and who reject the truth and follow evil, there will be wrath and anger.

Romans 2:7-8

Be devoted to one another in brotherly love. Honor one another above yourselves.

Romans 12:10

Give everyone what you owe him: If you owe taxes, pay taxes; if revenue, then revenue; if respect, then respect; if honor, then honor.

Romans 13:7

You were bought at a price. Therefore honor God with your body.

1 Corinthians 6:20

Honor your father and mother — which is the first commandment with a promise.

Ephesians 6:2

Obedience @ Work

But Samuel replied: "Does the LORD delight in burnt offerings and sacrifices as much as in obeying the voice of the LORD? To obey is better than sacrifice, and to heed is better than the fat of rams."

1 Samuel 15:22

But from everlasting to everlasting the LORD's love is with those who fear him, and his righteousness with their children's children — with those who keep his covenant and remember to obey his precepts.

Psalm 103:17-18

He who obeys instructions guards his life, but he who is contemptuous of his ways will die.

Proverbs 19:16

To do what is right and just is more acceptable to the LORD than sacrifice.

Proverbs 21:3

If you are willing and obedient, you will eat the best from the land; but if you resist and rebel, you will be devoured by the sword. For the mouth of he LORD has spoken.

Isaiah 1:19-20

He replied, "Blessed rather are those who hear the word of God and obey it."

Luke 11:28

Peter and the other apostles replied: We must obey God rather than men!

Acts 5:29

Slaves (employees), obey your earthly masters (employers) with respect and fear, and with sincerity of heart, just as you would obey Christ. Obey them not only to win their favor when their eye is on you, but like slaves (employees) of Christ, doing the will of God from your heart. Serve wholeheartedly, as if you were serving the Lord, not men, because you know that the Lord will reward everyone for whatever good he does, whether he is slave (employee) or free.

Ephesians 6:5-8

Slaves (employees), obey your earthly masters (employers) in everything; and do it, not only when their eye is on you and to win their favor, but with sincerity of heart and reverence for the Lord. Whatever you do, work at it with all your heart, as working for the Lord, not for men, since you know that you will receive an inheritance from the Lord as a reward. It is the Lord Christ you are serving.

Colossians 3:22-24

Those who have believing masters (employers) are not to show less respect for them because they are brothers. Instead, they are to serve them even better, because those who benefit from their service are believers, and dear to them. These are the things you are to teach and urge on them.

1 Timothy 6:2

Teach slaves (employees) to be subject to their masters (employers) in everything, to try to please them, not to talk back to them, and not to steal from them, but to show that they can be fully trusted, so that in every way they will make the teaching about God our Savior attractive.

Titus 2:9-10

Slaves (employees), submit yourselves to your masters (employers) with all respect, not only to those who are good and considerate, but also to those who are harsh.

1 Peter 2:18

We know that we have come to know him if we obey his commands. The man who says, I know him, but does not do what he commands is a liar, and the truth is not in him. But if anyone obeys his word, God's love is truly made complete in him. This is how we know we are in him: Whoever claims to live in him must walk as Jesus did.

1 John 2:3-6

The world and its desires pass away, but the man who does the will of God lives forever.

1 John 2:17

Loyalty @ Work

Godly Character @ Work

Do not blaspheme God or curse the ruler of your people.

Exodus 22:28

When the LORD was about to take Elijah up to heaven in a whirlwind, Elijah and Elisha were on their way from Gilgal. Elijah said to Elisha, "Stay here; the LORD has sent me to Bethel." But Elisha said, "As surely as the LORD lives and as you live, I will not leave you." So they went down to Bethel. The company of the prophets at Bethel came out to Elisha and asked, "Do you know that the LORD is going to take your master from you today?" "Yes, I know," Elisha replied, "but do not speak of it." Then Elijah said to him, "Stay here, Elisha; the LORD has sent me to Jericho." And he replied, "As surely as the LORD lives and as you live, I will not leave you." So they went to Jericho. The company of the prophets at Jericho went up to Elisha and asked him, "Do you know that the LORD is going to take your master from you today?" "Yes, I know, he replied, "But do not speak of it." Then Elijah said to him, "Stay here; the LORD has sent me to the Jordan." And he replied, "As surely as the LORD lives and as you live, I will not leave you." So the two of them walked on. Fifty men of the company of the prophets went and stood at a distance, facing the place where Elijah and Elisha had stopped at the Jordan. Elijah took his cloak, rolled it up and struck the water with it. The water divided to the right and to the left, and the two of them crossed over on dry ground. When they had crossed, Elijah said to Elisha, "Tell me, what can I do for you before I am taken from you?" "Let me inherit a double portion of your spirit," Elisha replied. "You have asked a difficult thing," Elijah said, "yet if you see me when I am taken from you, it will be yours — otherwise not."

As they were walking along and talking together, suddenly a chariot of fire and horses of fire appeared and separated the two of them, and Elijah went up to heaven in a whirlwind. Elisha saw this and cried out, "My father! My father! The chariots and horsemen of Israel!" And Elisha saw him no more. Then he took hold of his own clothes and tore them apart. He picked up the cloak that had fallen from Elijah and went back and stood on the bank of the Jordan. Then he took the cloak that had fallen from him and struck the water with it. "Where now is the LORD, the God of Elijah?" he asked. When he struck the water, it divided to the right and to the left, and he crossed over. The company of the prophets from Jericho, who were watching, said, "The spirit of Elijah is resting on Elisha." And they went to meet him and bowed to the ground before him.

2 Kings 2:1-15

Love the LORD, all his saints! The LORD preserves the faithful, but the proud he pays back in full.

Psalm 31:23

A gossip betrays a confidence, but a trustworthy man keeps a secret.

Proverbs 11:13

A wicked messenger falls into trouble, but a trustworthy envoy brings healing.

Proverbs 13:17

What a man desires is unfailing love; better to be poor than a liar.

Proverbs 19:22

Many a man claims to have unfailing love, but a faithful man who can find?

Proverbs 20:6

Fear the LORD and the king, my son, and do not join with the rebellious.

Proverbs 24:21

He who tends a fig tree will eat its fruit, and he who looks after his master will be honored.

Proverbs 27: 18

A faithful man will be richly blessed, but one eager to get rich will not go unpunished.

Proverbs 28:20

If a ruler's anger rises against you, do not leave your post; calmness can lay great errors to rest.

Ecclesiastes 10:4

Be devoted to one another in brotherly love. Honor one another above yourselves.

Romans 12:10

Everyone must submit himself to the governing authorities, for there is no authority except that which God has established. The authorities that exist have been established by God.

Romans 13:1

Moreover it is required in stewards that one be found faithful.

1 Corinthians 4:2 (NKJ)

Remind the people to be subject to rulers and authorities, to be obedient, to be ready to do whatever is good.

Titus 3:1

Patience @ Work

Godly Character @ Work

Wait for the LORD; be strong and take heart and wait for the LORD.

Psalm 27:14

Be still before the LORD and wait patiently for him; do not fret when men succeed in their ways, when they carry out their wicked schemes. Refrain from anger and turn from wrath; do not fret — it leads only to evil. For evil men will be cut off, but those who hope in the LORD will inherit the land.

Psalm 37:7-9

Wait for the LORD and keep his way. He will exalt you to inherit the land; when the wicked are cut off, you will see it.

Psalm 37:34

A patient man has great understanding, but a quick-tempered man displays folly.

Proverbs 14:29

A hot-tempered man stirs up dissension, but a patient man calms a quarrel.

Proverbs 15:18

Better a patient man than a warrior, a man who controls his temper than one who takes a city.

Proverbs 16:32

It is not good to have zeal without knowledge, nor to be hasty and miss the way.

Proverbs 19:2

A man's wisdom gives him patience; it is to his glory to overlook an offense.

Proverbs 19:11

Do not say, "I'll pay you back for this wrong!" Wait for the LORD, and he will deliver you.

Proverbs 20:22

Do not wear yourself out to get rich; have the wisdom to show restraint.

Proverbs 23:4

The end of a matter is better than its beginning, and patience is better than pride. Do not be quickly provoked in your spirit, for anger resides in the lap of fools.

Ecclesiastes 7:8-9

It is good to wait quietly for the salvation of the LORD. It is good for a man to bear the yoke while he is young.

Lamentations 3:26-27

But those who wait on the LORD shall renew their strength; they shall mount up with wings like eagles, they shall run and not be weary, they shall walk and not faint.

Isaiah 40:31 (NKJ)

But the seed on good soil stands for those with a noble and good heart, who hear the word, retain it, and by persevering produce a crop.

Luke 8:15

Not only so, but we also rejoice in our sufferings, because we know that suffering produces perseverance; character; and character, hope.

Romans 5:3-4

But if we hope for what we do not yet have, we wait for it patiently.

Romans 8:25

Be joyful in hope, patient in affliction, faithful in prayer.

Romans 12:12

For everything that was written in the past was written to teach us, so that through endurance and the encouragement of the Scriptures we might have hope. May the God who gives endurance and encouragement give you a spirit of unity among yourselves as you follow Christ Jesus,

Romans 15:4-5

Love is patient, love is kind. It does not envy, it does not boast, it is not proud. It is not rude, it is not self-seeking, it is not easily angered, it keeps no record of wrongs.

1 Corinthians 13:4-5

Let us not become weary in doing good, for at the proper time we will reap a harvest if we do not give up.

Galatians 6:9

As a prisoner for the Lord, then, I urge you to live a life worthy of the calling you have received. Be completely humble and gentle; be patient, bearing with one another in love.

Ephesians 4:1-2

And we pray this in order that you may live a life worthy of the Lord and may please him in every way: bearing fruit in every good work, growing in the knowledge of God, being strengthened with all power according to his glorious might so that you may have great endurance and patience, and joyfully.

Colossians 1:10-11

Therefore, as God's chosen people, holy and dearly loved, clothe yourselves with compassion, kindness, humility, gentleness and patience.
Bear with each other and forgive whatever grievances you may have
against one another. Forgive as the Lord forgave you.

Colossians 3:12-13

We continually remember before our God and Father your work produced
by faith, your labor prompted by love, and your endurance inspired by
hope in our Lord Jesus Christ.

1 Thessalonians 1:3

And we urge you, brothers, warn those who are idle, encourage the
timid, help the weak, be patient with everyone.

1 Thessalonians 5:14

May the Lord direct your hearts into God's love and Christ's perseverance.

2 Thessalonians 3:5

Now the overseer must be above reproach, the husband of but one wife,
temperate, self-controlled, respectable, hospitable, able to teach, not
given to drunkenness, not violent but gentle, not quarrelsome, not a
lover of money.

1 Timothy 3:2-3

But you, man of God, flee from all this, and pursue righteousness, godliness, faith, love, endurance and gentleness.

1 Timothy 6:11

And the Lord's servant must not quarrel; instead, he must be kind to
everyone, able to teach, not resentful. Those who oppose him he must
gently instruct, in the hope that God will grant them repentance leading
them to a knowledge of the truth,

2 Timothy 2:24-25

You must teach what is in accord with sound doctrine. Teach the older
men to be temperate, worthy of respect, self-controlled, and sound in
faith, in love and in endurance.

Titus 2:1-2

We do not want you to become lazy, but to imitate those who through faith and patience inherit what has been promised. And so after waiting patiently, Abraham received what was promised.

Hebrews 6:12,15

You need to persevere so that when you have done the will of God, you will receive what he has promised.

Hebrews 10:36

Therefore, since we are surrounded by such a great cloud of witnesses, let us throw off everything that hinders and the sin that so easily entangles, and let us run with perseverance the race marked out for us.

Hebrews 12:1

Because you know that the testing of your faith develops perseverance. Perseverance must finish its work so that you may be mature and complete, not lacking anything. My dear brothers, take note of this: Everyone should be quick to listen, slow to speak and slow to become angry.

James 1:3-4,19

Be patient, then, brothers, until the Lord's coming. See how the farmer waits for the land to yield its valuable crop and how patient he is for the autumn and spring rains. You too, be patient and stand firm, because the Lord's coming is near.

James 5:7-8

For it is commendable if a man bears up under the pain of unjust suffering because he is conscious of God. But how is it to your credit if you receive a beating for doing wrong and endure it? But if you suffer for doing good and you endure it, this is commendable before God. To this you were called, because Christ suffered for you, leaving you an example, that you should follow in his steps. He committed no sin, and no deceit was found in his mouth. When they hurled their insults at him, he did not retaliate; when he suffered, he made no threats. Instead, he entrusted himself to him who judges justly.

1 Peter 2:19-23

Self-Control @ Work

A fool shows his annoyance at once, but a prudent man overlooks an insult.

Proverbs 12:16

A patient man has great understanding, but a quick-tempered man displays folly.

Proverbs 14:29

Better a patient man than a warrior, a man who controls his temper than one who takes a city.

Proverbs 16:32

A hot-tempered man must pay the penalty; if you rescue him, you will have to do it again.

Proverbs 19:19

Do not make friends with a hot-tempered man, do not associate with one easily angered,

Proverbs 22:24

Like a city whose walls are broken down is a man who lacks self-control.

Proverbs 25:28

A fool gives full vent to his anger, but a wise man keeps himself under control.

Proverbs 29:11

Do you see a man who speaks in haste? There is more hope for a fool than for him.

Proverbs 29:20

But the fruit of the Spirit is love, joy, peace, patience, kindness, goodness, faithfulness, gentleness and self-control. Against such things there is no law.

Galatians 5:22-23

Finally, brothers, we instructed you how to live in order to please God, as in fact you are living. Now we ask you and urge you in the Lord Jesus to do this more and more. For you know what instructions we gave you by the authority of the Lord Jesus It is God's will that you should be sanctified: that you should avoid sexual immorality; that each of you should learn to control his own body in a way that is holy and honorable, not in passionate lust like the heathen, who do not know God; and that in this matter no one should wrong his brother or take advantage of him. The Lord will punish men for all such sins, as we have already told you and warned you. For God did not call us to be impure, but to live a holy life.

1 Thessalonians 4:1-7

You are all sons of the light and sons of the day. We do not belong to the night or to the darkness. So then, let us not be like others, who are asleep, but let us be alert and self-controlled. For those who sleep, sleep at night, and those who get drunk, get drunk at night. But since we belong to the day, let us be self-controlled, putting on faith and love as a breastplate, and the hope of salvation as a helmet.

1 Thessalonians 5:5-8

Now the overseer must be above reproach, the husband of but one wife, temperate, self-controlled, respectable, hospitable, able to teach.

1 Timothy 3:2

Since an overseer is entrusted with God's work, he must be blameless — not overbearing, not quick-tempered, not given to drunkenness, not violent, not pursuing dishonest gain. Rather he must be hospitable, one who loves what is good, who is self-controlled, upright, holy and disciplined.

Titus 1:7-8

Teach the older men to be temperate, worthy of respect, self-controlled, and sound in faith, in love and in endurance.

Titus 2:2

Likewise, teach the older women to be reverent in the way they live, not to be slanderers or addicted to much wine, but to teach what is good. Then they can train the younger women to love their husbands and children, to be self-controlled and pure, to be busy at home, to be kind, and to be subject to their husbands, so that no one will malign the word of God.

Titus 2:3-5

Similarly, encourage the young men to be self-controlled. In everything set them an example by doing what is good. In your teaching show integrity, seriousness.

Titus 2:6-7

It teaches us to say No to ungodliness and worldly passions, and to live self-controlled, upright and godly lives in this present age.

Titus 2:12

My dear brothers, take note of this: Everyone should be quick to listen, slow to speak and slow to become angry.

James 1:19

Therefore, prepare your minds for action; be self-controlled; set your hope fully on the grace to be given you when Jesus Christ is revealed. As obedient children, do not conform to the evil desires you had when you lived in ignorance. But just as he who called you is holy, so be holy in all you do; for it is written: "Be holy, because I am holy."

1 Peter 1:13-16

The end of all things is near. Therefore be clear minded and self-controlled so that you can pray.

1 Peter 4:7

Be self-controlled and alert. Your enemy the devil prowls around like a roaring lion looking for someone to devour. Resist him, standing firm in the faith, because you know that your brothers throughout the world are undergoing the same kind of sufferings.

1 Peter 5:8-9

His divine power has given us everything we need for life and godliness through our knowledge of him who called us by his own glory and goodness. Through these he has given us his very great and precious promises, so that through them you may participate in the divine nature and escape the corruption in the world caused by evil desires. For this very reason, make every effort to add to your faith goodness; and to goodness, knowledge; and to knowledge, self-control; and to self-control, perseverance; and to perseverance, godliness; and to godliness, brotherly kindness; and to brotherly kindness, love. For if you possess these qualities in increasing measure, they will keep you from being ineffective and unproductive in your knowledge of our Lord Jesus Christ.

2 Peter 1:3-8

Contentment @ Work

The LORD is my shepherd, I shall not be in want.

Psalm 23:1

Fear the LORD, you his saints, for those who fear him lack nothing.

Psalm 34:9

Trust in the LORD and do good; dwell in the land and enjoy safe pasture. Delight yourself in the LORD and he will give you the desires of your heart. Commit your way to the LORD; trust in him and he will do this: He will make your righteousness shine like the dawn, the justice of your cause like the noonday sun. Be still before the LORD and wait patiently for him; do not fret when men succeed in their ways, when they carry out their wicked schemes.

Psalm 37:3-7

Better the little that the righteous have than the wealth of many wicked; for the power of the wicked will be broken, but the LORD upholds the righteous.

Psalm 37:16-17

Trust in him at all times, O people; pour out your hearts to him, for God is our refuge. Selah.

Psalm 62:8

For the LORD God is a sun and shield; the LORD bestows favor and honor; no good thing does he withhold from those whose walk is blameless.

Psalm 84:11

Good will come to him who is generous and lends freely, who conducts his affairs with justice.

Psalm 112:5

Those who trust in the LORD are like Mount Zion, which cannot be shaken but endures forever. As the mountains surround Jerusalem, so the LORD surrounds his people both now and forevermore.

Psalm 125:1-2

Trust in the LORD with all your heart and lean not on your own understanding; in all your ways acknowledge him, and he will make your paths straight.

Proverbs 3:5-6

Better a little with the fear of the LORD than great wealth with turmoil.

Proverbs 15:16

Better a meal of vegetables where there is love than a fattened calf with hatred.

Proverbs 15:17

Better a little with righteousness than much gain with injustice.

Proverbs 16:8

Better a dry crust with peace and quiet than a house full of feasting, with strife.

Proverbs 17:1

Keep falsehood and lies far from me; give me neither poverty nor riches, but give me only my daily bread. Otherwise, I may have too much and disown you and say, "Who is the LORD?" Or I may become poor and steal, and so dishonor the name of my God.

Proverbs 30:8-9

A man can do nothing better than to eat and drink and find satisfaction in his work. This too, I see, is from the hand of God, for without him, who can eat or find enjoyment? To the man who pleases him, God gives wisdom, knowledge and happiness, but to the sinner he gives the task of gathering and storing up wealth to hand it over to the one who pleases God. This too is meaningless, a chasing after the wind.

Ecclesiastes 2:24-26

I know that there is nothing better for men than to be happy and do good while they live. That everyone may eat and drink, and find satisfaction in all his toil — this is the gift of God.

Ecclesiastes 3:12-13

Better one handful with tranquillity than two handfuls with toil and chasing after the wind.

Ecclesiastes 4:6

The sleep of a laborer is sweet, whether he eats little or much, but the abundance of a rich man permits him no sleep. I have seen a grievous evil under the sun: wealth hoarded to the harm of its owner, or wealth lost through some misfortune, so that when he has a son there is nothing left for him. Naked a man comes from his mother's womb, and as he comes, so he departs. He takes nothing from his labor that he can carry in his hand. This too is a grievous evil: As a man comes, so he departs, and what does he gain, since he toils for the wind?

Ecclesiastes 5:12-16

Then I realized that it is good and proper for a man to eat and drink, and to find satisfaction in his toilsome labor under the sun during the few days of life God has given him — for this is his lot. Moreover, when God gives any man wealth and possessions, and enables him to enjoy them, to accept his lot and be happy in his work — this is a gift of God. He seldom reflects on the days of his life, because God keeps him occupied with gladness of heart.

Ecclesiastes 5:18-20

So I commend the enjoyment of life, because nothing is better for a man under the sun than to eat and drink and be glad. Then joy will accompany him in his work all the days of the life God has given him under the sun.

Ecclesiastes 8:15

You will keep in perfect peace him whose mind is steadfast, because he trusts in you. Trust in the LORD forever, for the LORD, the LORD, is the Rock eternal.

Isaiah 26:3-4

But blessed is the man who trusts in the LORD, whose confidence is in him. He will be like a tree planted by the water that sends out its roots by the stream. It does not fear when heat comes; its leaves are always green. It has no worries in a year of drought and never fails to bear fruit.

Jeremiah 17:7-8

Therefore I tell you, do not worry about your life, what you will eat or drink; or about your body, what you will wear. Is not life more important than food, and the body more important than clothes? Look at the birds of the air; they do not sow or reap or store away in barns, and yet your heavenly Father feeds them. Are you not much more valuable than they? Who of you by worrying can add a single hour to his life? And why do you worry about clothes? See how the lilies of the field grow. They do not labor or spin. Yet I tell you that not even Solomon in all his splendor was dressed like one of these. If that is how God clothes the grass of the field, which is here today and tomorrow is thrown into the fire, will he not much more clothe you, O you of little faith? So do not worry, saying, What shall we eat? or What shall we drink? or What shall we wear? For the pagans run after all these things, and your heavenly Father knows that you need them. But seek first his kingdom and his righteousness, and all these things will be given to you as well. Therefore do not worry about tomorrow, for tomorrow will worry about itself. Each day has enough trouble of its own.

Matthew 6:25-34

Then some soldiers asked him, "And what should we do?" He replied, "Don't extort money and don't accuse people falsely — be content with your pay."

Luke 3:14

Therefore Jesus said again, "I tell you the truth, I am the gate for the sheep. All who ever came before me were thieves and robbers, but the sheep did not listen to them. I am the gate; whoever enters through me will be saved. He will come in and go out, and find pasture. The thief comes only to steal and kill and destroy; I have come that they may have life, and have it to the full."

John 10:7-10

What, then, shall we say in response to this? If God is for us, who can be against us? He who did not spare his own Son, but gave him up for us all — how will he not also, along with him, graciously give us all things?

Romans 8:31-32

Remember this: Whoever sows sparingly will also reap sparingly, and whoever sows generously will also reap generously. Each man should give what he has decided in his heart to give, not reluctantly or under compulsion, for God loves a cheerful giver. And God is able to make all grace abound to you, so that in all things at all times, having all that you need, you will abound in every good work.

2 Corinthians 9:6-8

We do not dare to classify or compare ourselves with some who commend themselves. When they measure themselves by themselves and compare themselves with themselves, they are not wise.

2 Corinthians 10:12

I am not saying this because I am in need, for I have learned to be content whatever the circumstances. I know what it is to be in need, and I know what it is to have plenty. I have learned the secret of being content in any and every situation, whether well fed or hungry, whether living in plenty or in want. I can do everything through him who gives me strength.

Philippians 4:11-13

And my God will meet all your needs according to his glorious riches in
Christ Jesus.

Philippians 4:19

But godliness with contentment is great gain. For we brought nothing
into the world, and we can take nothing out of it. But if we have food
and clothing, we will be content with that. People who want to get rich
fall into temptation and a trap and into many foolish and harmful desires that plunge men into ruin and destruction. For the love of money
is a root of all kinds of evil. Some people, eager for money, have wandered from the faith and pierced themselves with many griefs. But you,
man of God, flee from all this, and pursue righteousness, godliness,
faith, love, endurance and gentleness.

1 Timothy 6:6-11

Keep your lives free from the love of money and be content with what
you have, because God has said, "Never will I leave you; never will I
forsake you."

Hebrews 13:5

Kindness @ Work

If you see your brother's ox or sheep straying, do not ignore it but be sure to take it back to him. If the brother does not live near you or if you do not know who he is, take it home with you and keep it until he comes looking for it. Then give it back to him. Do the same if you find your brother's donkey or his cloak or anything he loses. Do not ignore it. If you see your brother's donkey or his ox fallen on the road, do not ignore it. Help him get it to its feet.

Deuteronomy 22:1-4

Good will come to him who is generous and lends freely, who conducts his affairs with justice.

Psalm 112:5

A kindhearted woman gains respect, but ruthless men gain only wealth. A kind man benefits himself, but a cruel man brings trouble on himself.

Proverbs 11:16-17

A righteous man cares for the needs of his animal, but the kindest acts of the wicked are cruel.

Proverbs 12:10

An anxious heart weighs a man down, but a kind word cheers him up.

Proverbs 12:25

He who despises his neighbor sins, but blessed is he who is kind to the needy.

Proverbs 14:21

He who oppresses the poor shows contempt for their Maker, but whoever is kind to the needy honors God.

Proverbs 14:31

He who is kind to the poor lends to the LORD, and he will reward him for what he has done.

Proverbs 19:17

He who increases his wealth by exorbitant interest amasses it for another, who will be kind to the poor.

Proverbs 28:8

"This is what the LORD Almighty says: 'Administer true justice; show mercy and compassion to one another.'"

Zechariah 7:9

Blessed are the merciful, for they will be shown mercy.

Matthew 5:7

"Then the King will say to those on his right, 'Come, you who are blessed by my Father; take your inheritance, the kingdom prepared for you since the creation of the world. For I was hungry and you gave me something to eat, I was thirsty and you gave me something to drink, I was a stranger and you invited me in, I needed clothes and you clothed me, I was sick and you looked after me, I was in prison and you came to visit me.' Then the righteous will answer him, 'Lord, when did we see you hungry and feed you, or thirsty and give you something to drink? When did we see you a stranger and invite you in, or needing clothes and clothe you? When did we see you sick or in prison and go to visit you.' The King will reply, 'I tell you the truth, whatever you did for one of the least of these brothers of mine, you did for me.'"

Matthew 25:34-40

Give to everyone who asks you, and if anyone takes what belongs to you, do not demand it back. Do to others as you would have them do to you. If you love those who love you, what credit is that to you? Even sinners love those who love them. And if you do good to those who are good to you, what credit is that to you? Even sinners do that. And if you lend to those from whom you expect repayment, what credit is that to you? Even sinners lend to sinners, expecting to be repaid in full. But love your enemies, do good to them, and lend to them without expecting to get anything back. Then your reward will be great, and you will be sons of the Most High, because he is kind to the ungrateful and wicked. Be merciful, just as your Father is merciful.

Luke 6:30-36

Love is patient, love is kind. It does not envy, it does not boast, it is not proud.

1 Corinthians 13:4

Therefore, as we have opportunity, let us do good to all people, especially to those who belong to the family of believers.

Galatians 6:10

Be kind and compassionate to one another, forgiving each other, just as in Christ God forgave you.

Ephesians 4:32

Therefore, as God's chosen people, holy and dearly loved, clothe yourselves with compassion, kindness, humility, gentleness and patience. Bear with each other and forgive whatever grievances you may have against one another. Forgive as the Lord forgave you. And over all these virtues put on love, which binds them all together in perfect unity.

Colossians 3:12-14

Make sure that nobody pays back wrong for wrong, but always try to be kind to each other and to everyone else.

1 Thessalonians 5:15

Finally, all of you, live in harmony with one another; be sympathetic, love as brothers, be compassionate and humble. Do not repay evil with

evil or insult with insult, but with blessing, because to this you were
called so that you may inherit a blessing.

1 Peter 3:8-9

Above all, love each other deeply, because love covers over a multitude
of sins. Offer hospitality to one another without grumbling. Each one
should use whatever gift he has received to serve others, faithfully administering God's grace in its various forms.

1 Peter 4:8-10

For this very reason, make every effort to add to your faith goodness;
and to goodness, knowledge; and to knowledge, self-control; and to
self-control, perseverance; and to perseverance, godliness; and to godliness, brotherly kindness; and to brotherly kindness, love. For if you
possess these qualities in increasing measure, they will keep you from
being ineffective and unproductive in your knowledge of our Lord Jesus
Christ. But if anyone does not have them, he is nearsighted and blind,
and has forgotten that he has been cleansed from his past sins.

2 Peter 1:5-9

If anyone has material possessions and sees his brother in need but has
no pity on him, how can the love of God be in him?

1 John 3:17

Generosity @ Work

If there is a poor man among your brothers in any of the towns of the land that the LORD your God is giving you, do not be hardhearted or tightfisted toward your poor brother. Rather be openhanded and freely lend him whatever he needs.

Deuteronomy 15:7-8

When you are harvesting in your field and you overlook a sheaf, do not go back to get it. Leave it for the alien, the fatherless and the widow, so that the LORD your God may bless you in all the work of your hands. When you beat the olives from your trees, do not go over the branches a second time. Leave what remains for the alien, the fatherless and the widow. When you harvest the grapes in your vineyard, do not go over the vines again. Leave what remains for the alien, the fatherless and the widow.

Deuteronomy 24:19-21

Good will come to him who is generous and lends freely, who conducts his affairs with justice. Surely he will never be shaken; a righteous man will be remembered forever. He will have no fear of bad news; his heart is steadfast, trusting in the LORD. His heart is secure, he will have no fear; in the end he will look in triumph on his foes. He has scattered abroad his gifts to the poor, his righteousness endures forever; his horn will be lifted high in honor.

Psalm 112:5-9

Honor the LORD with your wealth, with the firstfruits of all your crops.

Proverbs 3:9

One man gives freely, yet gains even more; another withholds unduly, but comes to poverty.

Proverbs 11:24

A generous man will prosper; he who refreshes others will himself be refreshed.

Proverbs 11:25

He who despises his neighbor sins, but blessed is he who is kind to the needy.

Proverbs 14:21

He who is kind to the poor lends to the LORD, and he will reward him for what he has done.

Proverbs 19:17

If a man shuts his ears to the cry of the poor, he too will cry out and not be answered.

Proverbs 21:13

All day long he craves for more, but the righteous give without sparing.

Proverbs 21:26

A generous man will himself be blessed, for he shares his food with the poor.

Proverbs 22:9

A stingy man is eager to get rich and is unaware that poverty awaits him.

Proverbs 28:22

He who gives to the poor will lack nothing, but he who closes his eyes to them receives many curses.

Proverbs 28:27

Give to the one who asks you, and do not turn away from the one who
wants to borrow from you.

Matthew 5:42

Be careful not to do your acts of righteousness before men, to be seen
by them. If you do, you will have no reward from your Father in heaven.
So when you give to the needy, do not announce it with trumpets, as
the hypocrites do in the synagogues and on the streets, to be honored
by men. I tell you the truth, they have received their reward in full. But
when you give to the needy, do not let your left hand know what your
right hand is doing, so that your giving may be in secret. Then your
Father, who sees what is done in secret, will reward you.

Matthew 6:1-4

"What should we do then?" the crowd asked. John answered, "The man
with two tunics should share with him who has none, and the one who
has food should do the same."

Luke 3:10-11

Give, and it will be given to you. A good measure, pressed down, shaken
together and running over, will be poured into your lap. For with the
measure you use, it will be measured to you.

Luke 6:38

All the believers were one in heart and mind. No one claimed that any of
his possessions was his own, but they shared everything they had.

Acts 4:32

Cornelius stared at him in fear. "What is it, Lord?" he asked. The angel
answered, "Your prayers and gifts to the poor have come up as a memo-
rial offering before God."

Acts 10:4

In everything I did, I showed you that by this kind of hard work we must
help the weak, remembering the words the Lord Jesus himself said: "It
is more blessed to give than to receive."

Acts 20:35

Share with God's people who are in need. Practice hospitality.

Romans 12:13

But just as you excel in everything — in faith, in speech, in knowledge, in complete earnestness and in your love for us — see that you also excel in this grace of giving.

2 Corinthians 8:7

Remember this: Whoever sows sparingly will also reap sparingly, and whoever sows generously will also reap generously. Each man should give what he has decided in his heart to give, not reluctantly or under compulsion, for God loves a cheerful giver. And God is able to make all grace abound to you, so that in all things at all times, having all that you need, you will abound in every good work. As it is written: "He has scattered abroad his gifts to the poor; his righteousness endures forever." Now he who supplies seed to the sower and bread for food will also supply and increase your store of seed and will enlarge the harvest of your righteousness. You will be made rich in every way so that you can be generous on every occasion, and through us your generosity will result in thanksgiving to God. This service that you perform is not only supplying the needs of God's people but is also overflowing in many expressions of thanks to God. Because of the service by which you have proved yourselves, men will praise God for the obedience that accompanies your confession of the gospel of Christ, and for your generosity in sharing with them and with everyone else.

2 Corinthians 9:6-13

He who has been stealing must steal no longer, but must work, doing something useful with his own hands, that he may have something to share with those in need.

Ephesians 4:28

Command those who are rich in this present world not to be arrogant nor to put their hope in wealth, which is so uncertain, but to put their hope in God, who richly provides us with everything for our enjoyment. Command them to do good, to be rich in good deeds, and to be generous and willing to share. In this way they will lay up treasure for themselves as a firm foundation for the coming age, so that they may take hold of the life that is truly life.

1 Timothy 6:17-19

And do not forget to do good and to share with others, for with such sacrifices God is pleased.

Hebrews 13:16

If anyone has material possessions and sees his brother in need but has no pity on him, how can the love of God be in him? Dear children, let us not love with words or tongue but with actions and in truth.

1 John 3:17-18

Foolishness @ Work

Resentment kills a fool, and envy slays the simple.

Job 5:2

I myself have seen a fool taking root, but suddenly his house was cursed.

Job 5:3

The fool says in his heart, "There is no God." They are corrupt, their deeds are vile; there is no one who does good.

Psalm 14:1

The fear of the LORD is the beginning of knowledge, but fools despise wisdom and discipline.

Proverbs 1:7

The wise in heart accept commands, but a chattering fool comes to ruin.

Proverbs 10:8

Wise men store up knowledge, but the mouth of a fool invites ruin.

Proverbs 10:14

He who conceals his hatred has lying lips, and whoever spreads slander is a fool.

Proverbs 10:18

The lips of the righteous nourish many, but fools die for lack of judgment.

Proverbs 10:21

A fool finds pleasure in evil conduct, but a man of understanding delights in wisdom.

Proverbs 10:23

He who brings trouble on his family will inherit only wind, and the fool will be servant to the wise.

Proverbs 11:29

The way of a fool seems right to him, but a wise man listens to advice.

Proverbs 12:15

A fool shows his annoyance at once, but a prudent man overlooks an insult.

Proverbs 12:16

A prudent man keeps his knowledge to himself, but the heart of fools blurts out folly.

Proverbs 12:23

Every prudent man acts out of knowledge, but a fool exposes his folly.

Proverbs 13:16

A longing fulfilled is sweet to the soul, but fools detest turning from evil.

Proverbs 13:19

He who walks with the wise grows wise, but a companion of fools suffers harm.

Proverbs 13:20

A fool's talk brings a rod to his back, but the lips of the wise protect them.

Proverbs 14:3

Stay away from a foolish man, for you will not find knowledge on his lips.

Proverbs 14:7

The wisdom of the prudent is to give thought to their ways, but the folly of fools is deception.

Proverbs 14:8

Fools mock at making amends for sin, but goodwill is found among the upright.

Proverbs 14:9

A wise man fears the LORD and shuns evil, but a fool is hotheaded and reckless.

Proverbs 14:16

A quick-tempered man does foolish things, and a crafty man is hated.

Proverbs 14:17

The wealth of the wise is their crown, but the folly of fools yields folly.

Proverbs 14:24

A fool spurns his father's discipline, but whoever heeds correction shows prudence.

Proverbs 15:5

The lips of the wise spread knowledge; not so the hearts of fools.

Proverbs 15:7

Understanding is a fountain of life to those who have it, but folly brings punishment to fools.

Proverbs 16:22

A rebuke impresses a man of discernment more than a hundred lashes a fool.

Proverbs 17:10

Better to meet a bear robbed of her cubs than a fool in his folly.

Proverbs 17:12

Of what use is money in the hand of a fool, since he has no desire to get wisdom?

Proverbs 17:16

To have a fool for a son brings grief; there is no joy for the father of a fool.

Proverbs 17:21

A discerning man keeps wisdom in view, but a fool's eyes wander to the ends of the earth.

Proverbs 17:24

A foolish son brings grief to his father and bitterness to the one who bore him.

Proverbs 17:25

A fool finds no pleasure in understanding but delights in airing his own opinions.

Proverbs 18:2

A fool's lips bring him strife, and his mouth invites a beating.

Proverbs 18:6

A fool's mouth is his undoing, and his lips are a snare to his soul.

Proverbs 18:7

Better a poor man whose walk is blameless than a fool whose lips are perverse.

Proverbs 19:1

It is not fitting for a fool to live in luxury — how much worse for a slave to rule over princes!

Proverbs 19:10

A foolish son is his father's ruin, and a quarrelsome wife is like a constant dripping.

Proverbs 19:13

Penalties are prepared for mockers, and beatings for the backs of fools.

Proverbs 19:29

It is to a man's honor to avoid strife, but every fool is quick to quarrel.

Proverbs 20:3

In the house of the wise are stores of choice food and oil, but a foolish man devours all he has.

Proverbs 21:20

Do not speak to a fool, for he will scorn the wisdom of your words.

Proverbs 23:9

Like snow in summer or rain in harvest, honor is not fitting for a fool.

Proverbs 26:1

A whip for the horse, a halter for the donkey, and a rod for the backs of fools!

Proverbs 26:3

Do not answer a fool according to his folly, or you will be like him yourself.

Proverbs 26:4

Like cutting off one's feet or drinking violence is the sending of a message by the hand of a fool. Like a lame man's legs that hang limp is a proverb in the mouth of a fool. Like tying a stone in a sling is the giving of honor to a fool. Like a thornbush in a drunkard's hand is a proverb in the mouth of a fool. Like an archer who wounds at random is he who hires a fool or any passer-by. As a dog returns to its vomit, so a fool repeats his folly.

Proverbs 26:6-11

Do you see a man wise in his own eyes? There is more hope for a fool than for him.

Proverbs 26:12

Stone is heavy and sand a burden, but provocation by a fool is heavier than both.

Proverbs 27:1

Though you grind a fool in a mortar, grinding him like grain with a pestle, you will not remove his folly from him.

Proverbs 27:22

If a wise man goes to court with a fool, the fool rages and scoffs, and there is no peace.

Proverbs 29:9

A fool gives full vent to his anger, but a wise man keeps himself under control.

Proverbs 29:11

If you have played the fool and exalted yourself, or if you have planned evil, clap your hand over your mouth!

Proverbs 30:32

The fool folds his hands and ruins himself.

Ecclesiastes 4:5

Extortion turns a wise man into a fool, and a bribe corrupts the heart.

Ecclesiastes 7:7

Do not be overwicked, and do not be a fool — why die before your time?

Ecclesiastes 7:17

Even as he walks along the road, the fool lacks sense and shows everyone how stupid he is.

Ecclesiastes 10:3

And the fool multiplies words. No one knows what is coming — who can tell him what will happen after him? A fool's work wearies him; he does not know the way to town.

Ecclesiastes 10:14-15

For the fool speaks folly, his mind is busy with evil: He practices ungod-liness and spreads error concerning the LORD; the hungry he leaves empty and from the thirsty he withholds water.

Isaiah 32:6

Part Three

Ethical Challenges @ Work

Asked to Do Something Unethical @ Work

If anyone sins and is unfaithful to the LORD by deceiving his neighbor about something entrusted to him or left in his care or stolen, or if he cheats him, or if he finds lost property and lies about it, or if he swears falsely, or if he commits any such sin that people may do — when he thus sins and becomes guilty, he must return what he has stolen or taken by extortion, or what was entrusted to him, or the lost property he found, or whatever it was he swore falsely about. He must make restitution in full, add a fifth of the value to it and give it all to the owner on the day he presents his guilt offering. And as a penalty he must bring to the priest, that is, to the LORD, his guilt offering, a ram from the flock, one without defect and of the proper value. In this way the priest will make atonement for him before the LORD, and he will be forgiven for any of these things he did that made him guilty.

Leviticus 6:2-7

Do not steal. Do not lie. Do not deceive one another.

Leviticus 19:11

My lips will not speak wickedness, and my tongue will utter no deceit.

Job 27:4

You destroy those who tell lies; bloodthirsty and deceitful men the LORD abhors.

Psalm 5:6

Why do you boast of evil, you mighty man? Why do you boast all day long, you who are a disgrace in the eyes of God? Your tongue plots destruction; it is like a sharpened razor, you who practice deceit. You love evil rather than good, falsehood rather than speaking the truth. Selah You love every harmful word, O you deceitful tongue! Surely God will bring you down to everlasting ruin: He will snatch you up and tear you from your tent; he will uproot you from the land of the living. Selah.

Psalm 52:1-5

But you, O God, will bring down the wicked into the pit of corruption; bloodthirsty and deceitful men will not live out half their days. But as for me, I trust in you.

Psalm 55:23

No one who practices deceit will dwell in my house; no one who speaks falsely will stand in my presence.

Psalm 101:7

Keep me from deceitful ways; be gracious to me through your law.
I have chosen the way of truth; I have set my heart on your laws.

Psalm 119:29-30

I hate and abhor falsehood but I love your law.

Psalm 119:163

Save me, O LORD, from lying lips and from deceitful tongues.

Psalm 120:2

Wisdom will save you from the ways of wicked men, from men whose words are perverse, who leave the straight paths to walk in dark ways, who delight in doing wrong and rejoice in the perverseness of evil, whose paths are crooked and who are devious in their ways.

Proverbs 2:12-15

The man of integrity walks securely, but he who takes crooked paths will be found out.

Proverbs 10:9

The LORD abhors dishonest scales, but accurate weights are his delight.

Proverbs 11:1

The integrity of the upright guides them, but the unfaithful are destroyed by their duplicity.

Proverbs 11:3

The wicked man earns deceptive wages, but he who sows righteousness reaps a sure reward.

Proverbs 11:18

The LORD detests men of perverse heart but he delights in those whose ways are blameless.

Proverbs 11:20

A good man obtains favor from the LORD, but the LORD condemns a crafty man.

Proverbs 12:2

There is deceit in the hearts of those who plot evil, but joy for those who promote peace.

Proverbs 12:20

The LORD detests lying lips, but he delights in men who are truthful.

Proverbs 12:22

One man pretends to be rich, yet has nothing; another pretends to be poor, yet has great wealth.

Proverbs 13:7

Dishonest money dwindles away, but he who gathers money little by little makes it grow.

Proverbs 13:11

A truthful witness does not deceive, but a false witness pours out lies.

Proverbs 14:5

A quick-tempered man does foolish things, and a crafty man is hated.

Proverbs 14:7

The wisdom of the prudent is to give thought to their ways, but the folly of fools is deception.

Proverbs 14:8

A truthful witness saves lives, but a false witness is deceitful.

Proverbs 14:25

The eyes of the LORD are everywhere, keeping watch on the wicked and the good.

Proverbs 15:3

The tongue that brings healing is a tree of life, but a deceitful tongue crushes the spirit.

Proverbs 15:4

Better a little with righteousness than much gain with injustice.

Proverbs 16:8

A man of perverse heart does not prosper; he whose tongue is deceitful falls into trouble.

Proverbs 17:20

Differing weights and differing measures — the LORD detests them both.

Proverbs 20:10

"It's no good, it's no good!" says the buyer; then off he goes and boasts about his purchase.

Proverbs 20:14

Food gained by fraud tastes sweet to a man, but he ends up with a mouth full of gravel.

Proverbs 20:17

The LORD detests differing weights, and dishonest scales do not please him.

Proverbs 20:23

A fortune made by a lying tongue is a fleeting vapor and a deadly snare.

Proverbs 21:6

Like a madman shooting firebrands or deadly arrows is a man who deceives his neighbor and says, "I was only joking!"

Proverbs 26:18-19

A malicious man disguises himself with his lips, but in his heart he harbors deceit. Though his speech is charming, do not believe him, for seven abominations fill his heart. His malice may be concealed by deception, but his wickedness will be exposed in the assembly.

Proverbs 26:24-26

He who leads the upright along an evil path will fall into his own trap, but the blameless will receive a good inheritance.

Proverbs 28:10

To show partiality is not good — yet a man will do wrong for a piece of bread.

Proverbs 28:21

Deception @ Work

If anyone sins and is unfaithful to the LORD by deceiving his neighbor about something entrusted to him or left in his care or stolen, or if he cheats him, or if he finds lost property and lies about it, or if he swears falsely, or if he commits any such sin that people may do — when he thus sins and becomes guilty, he must return what he has stolen or taken by extortion, or what was entrusted to him, or the lost property he found, or whatever it was he swore falsely about. He must make restitution in full, add a fifth of the value to it and give it all to the owner on the day he presents his guilt offering. And as a penalty he must bring to the priest, that is, to the LORD, his guilt offering, a ram from the flock, one without defect and of the proper value. In this way the priest will make atonement for him before the LORD, and he will be forgiven for any of these things he did that made him guilty.

Leviticus 6:2-7

Do not steal. Do not lie. Do not deceive one another.

Leviticus 19:11

My lips will not speak wickedness, and my tongue will utter no deceit.

Job 27:4

You destroy those who tell lies; bloodthirsty and deceitful men the LORD abhors.

Psalm 5:6

Why do you boast of evil, you mighty man? Why do you boast all day long, you who are a disgrace in the eyes of God? Your tongue plots destruction; it is like a sharpened razor, you who practice deceit. You love evil rather than good, falsehood rather than speaking the truth. Selah You love every harmful word, O you deceitful tongue! Surely God will bring you down to everlasting ruin: He will snatch you up and tear you from your tent; he will uproot you from the land of the living. Selah.

Psalm 52:1-5

But you, O God, will bring down the wicked into the pit of corruption; bloodthirsty and deceitful men will not live out half their days. But as for me, I trust in you.

Psalm 55:23

No one who practices deceit will dwell in my house; no one who speaks falsely will stand in my presence.

Psalm 101:7

Keep me from deceitful ways; be gracious to me through your law. I have chosen the way of truth; I have set my heart on your laws.

Psalm 119:29-30

I hate and abhor falsehood but I love your law.

Psalm 119:163

Save me, O LORD, from lying lips and from deceitful tongues.

Psalm 120:2

Wisdom will save you from the ways of wicked men, from men whose words are perverse, who leave the straight paths to walk in dark ways, who delight in doing wrong and rejoice in the perverseness of evil, whose paths are crooked and who are devious in their ways.

Proverbs 2:12-15

The man of integrity walks securely, but he who takes crooked paths will be found out.

Proverbs 10:9

The LORD abhors dishonest scales, but accurate weights are his delight.

Proverbs 11:1

The integrity of the upright guides them, but the unfaithful are destroyed by their duplicity.

Proverbs 11:3

The wicked man earns deceptive wages, but he who sows righteousness reaps a sure reward.

Proverbs 11:18

The LORD detests men of perverse heart but he delights in those whose ways are blameless.

Proverbs 11:20

A good man obtains favor from the LORD, but the LORD condemns a crafty man.

Proverbs 12:2

There is deceit in the hearts of those who plot evil, but joy for those who promote peace.

Proverbs 12:20

The LORD detests lying lips, but he delights in men who are truthful.

Proverbs 12:22

One man pretends to be rich, yet has nothing; another pretends to be poor, yet has great wealth.

Proverbs 13:7

Dishonest money dwindles away, but he who gathers money little by little makes it grow.

Proverbs 13:11

A truthful witness does not deceive, but a false witness pours out lies.

Proverbs 14:5

A quick-tempered man does foolish things, and a crafty man is hated.

Proverbs 14:7

The wisdom of the prudent is to give thought to their ways, but the folly of fools is deception.

Proverbs 14:8

A truthful witness saves lives, but a false witness is deceitful.

Proverbs 14:25

The eyes of the LORD are everywhere, keeping watch on the wicked and the good.

Proverbs 15:3

The tongue that brings healing is a tree of life, but a deceitful tongue crushes the spirit.

Proverbs 15:4

Better a little with righteousness than much gain with injustice.

Proverbs 16:8

A man of perverse heart does not prosper; he whose tongue is deceitful falls into trouble.

Proverbs 17:20

Differing weights and differing measures — the LORD detests them both.

Proverbs 20:10

"It's no good, it's no good!" says the buyer; then off he goes and boasts about his purchase.

Proverbs 20:14

Food gained by fraud tastes sweet to a man, but he ends up with a mouth full of gravel.

Proverbs 20:17

The LORD detests differing weights, and dishonest scales do not please him.

Proverbs 20:23

A fortune made by a lying tongue is a fleeting vapor and a deadly snare.

Proverbs 21:6

Like a madman shooting firebrands or deadly arrows is a man who deceives his neighbor and says, "I was only joking!"

Proverbs 26:18-19

A malicious man disguises himself with his lips, but in his heart he harbors deceit. Though his speech is charming, do not believe him, for seven abominations fill his heart. His malice may be concealed by deception, but his wickedness will be exposed in the assembly.

Proverbs 26:24-26

He who leads the upright along an evil path will fall into his own trap, but the blameless will receive a good inheritance.

Proverbs 28:10

To show partiality is not good — yet a man will do wrong for a piece of bread.

Proverbs 28:21

Lying @ Work

Ethical Challenges @ Work

You shall not give false testimony against your neighbor.

Exodus 20:16

Do not spread false reports. Do not help a wicked man by being a malicious witness.

Exodus 23:1

If anyone sins and is unfaithful to the LORD by deceiving his neighbor about something entrusted to him or left in his care or stolen, or if he cheats him, or if he finds lost property and lies about it, or if he swears falsely, or if he commits any such sin that people may do — when he thus sins and becomes guilty, he must return what he has stolen or taken by extortion, or what was entrusted to him, or the lost property he found, or whatever it was he swore falsely about. He must make restitution in full, add a fifth of the value to it and give it all to the owner on the day he presents his guilt offering. And as a penalty he must bring to the priest, that is, to the LORD, his guilt offering, a ram from the flock, one without defect and of the proper value.

Leviticus 6:2-6

Do not steal. Do not lie. Do not deceive one another.

Leviticus 19:11

My lips will not speak wickedness, and my tongue will utter no deceit.

Job 27:4

You destroy those who tell lies; bloodthirsty and deceitful men the LORD abhors.

Psalm 5:6

Keep your tongue from evil and your lips from speaking lies. Turn from evil and do good; seek peace and pursue it.

Psalm 34:13-14

Why do you boast of evil, you mighty man? Why do you boast all day long, you who are a disgrace in the eyes of God? Your tongue plots destruction; it is like a sharpened razor, you who practice deceit. You love evil rather than good, falsehood rather than speaking the truth. Selah. You love every harmful word, O you deceitful tongue! Surely God will bring you down to everlasting ruin: He will snatch you up and tear you from your tent; he will uproot you from the land of the living. Selah.

Psalm 52:1-5

But the king will rejoice in God; all who swear by God's name will praise him, while the mouths of liars will be silenced.

Psalm 63:11

Whoever slanders his neighbor in secret, him will I put to silence; whoever has haughty eyes and a proud heart, him will I not endure.

Psalm 101:5

No one who practices deceit will dwell in my house; no one who speaks falsely will stand in my presence.

Psalm 101:7

There are six things the LORD hates, seven that are detestable to him: haughty eyes, a lying tongue, hands that shed innocent blood, a heart that devises wicked schemes, feet that are quick to rush into evil, a false witness who pours out lies and a man who stirs up dissension among brothers.

Proverbs 6:16-19

A truthful witness gives honest testimony, but a false witness tells lies.

Proverbs 12:17

Truthful lips endure forever, but a lying tongue lasts only a moment.

Proverbs 12:19

The LORD detests lying lips, but he delights in men who are truthful.

Proverbs 12:22

A truthful witness does not deceive, but a false witness pours out lies.

Proverbs 14:5

Arrogant lips are unsuited to a fool — how much worse lying lips to a ruler!

Proverbs 17:7

A false witness will not go unpunished, and he who pours out lies will not go free.

Proverbs 19:5

What a man desires is unfailing love; better to be poor than a liar.

Proverbs 19:22

A corrupt witness mocks at justice, and the mouth of the wicked gulps down evil.

Proverbs 19:28

"It's no good, it's no good!" says the buyer; then off he goes and boasts about his purchase.

Proverbs 20:14

Food gained by fraud tastes sweet to a man, but he ends up with a mouth full of gravel.

Proverbs 20:17

A fortune made by a lying tongue is a fleeting vapor and a deadly snare.

Proverbs 21:6

A false witness will perish, and whoever listens to him will be destroyed forever.

Proverbs 21:28

Do not testify against your neighbor without cause, or use your lips to deceive.

Proverbs 24:28

Like a club or a sword or a sharp arrow is the man who gives false testimony against his neighbor.

Proverbs 25:18

A lying tongue hates those it hurts, and a flattering mouth works ruin.

Proverbs 26:28

Keep falsehood and lies far from me; give me neither poverty nor riches, but give me only my daily bread. Otherwise, I may have too much and disown you and say, "Who is the LORD?" Or I may become poor and steal, and so dishonor the name of my God.

Proverbs 30:8-9

Do not let your mouth lead you into sin. And do not protest to the messenger, My vow was a mistake. Why should God be angry at what you say and destroy the work of your hands?

Ecclesiastes 5:6

The scoundrel's methods are wicked, he makes up evil schemes to destroy the poor with lies, even when the plea of the needy is just. But the noble man makes noble plans, and by noble deeds he stands.

Isaiah 32:7-8

And he said to me, "This is the curse that is going out over the whole land; for according to what it says on one side, every thief will be banished, and according to what it says on the other, everyone who swears falsely will be banished."

Zechariah 5:3

You belong to your father, the devil, and you want to carry out your father's desire. He was a murderer from the beginning, not holding to the truth, for there is no truth in him. When he lies, he speaks his native language, for he is a liar and the father of lies.

John 8:44

Rather, we have renounced secret and shameful ways; we do not use deception, nor do we distort the word of God. On the contrary, by setting forth the truth plainly we commend ourselves to every man's conscience in the sight of God.

2 Corinthians 4:2

Therefore each of you must put off falsehood and speak truthfully to his neighbor, for we are all members of one body.

Ephesians 4:25

Do not let any unwholesome talk come out of your mouths, but only what is helpful for building others up according to their needs, that it may benefit those who listen.

Ephesians 4:29

Do not lie to each other, since you have taken off your old self with its practices and have put on the new self, which is being renewed in knowledge in the image of its Creator.

Colossians 3:9-10

For, Whoever would love life and see good days must keep his tongue from evil and his lips from deceitful speech.

1 Peter 3:10

But the cowardly, the unbelieving, the vile, the murderers, the sexually immoral, those who practice magic arts, the idolaters and all liars — their place will be in the fiery lake of burning sulfur. This is the second death.

Revelation 21:8

Stealing @ Work

You shall not steal.

Exodus 20:15

If a man steals an ox or a sheep and slaughters it or sells it, he must pay back five head of cattle for the ox and four sheep for the sheep. If a thief is caught breaking in and is struck so that he dies, the defender is not guilty of bloodshed; but if it happens after sunrise, he is guilty of bloodshed. A thief must certainly make restitution, but if he has nothing, he must be sold to pay for his theft. If the stolen animal is found alive in his possession — whether ox or donkey or sheep — he must pay back double.

Exodus 22:1-4

If anyone sins and is unfaithful to the LORD by deceiving his neighbor about something entrusted to him or left in his care or stolen, or if he cheats him, or if he finds lost property and lies about it, or if he swears falsely, or if he commits any such sin that people may do — when he thus sins and becomes guilty, he must return what he has stolen or taken by extortion, or what was entrusted to him, or the lost property he found, or whatever it was he swore falsely about. He must make restitution in full, add a fifth of the value to it and give it all to the owner on the day he presents his guilt offering.

Leviticus 6:2-5

Do not defraud your neighbor or rob him. Do not hold back the wages of a hired man overnight.

Leviticus 9:13

Do not steal. Do not lie. Do not deceive one another.

Leviticus 19:11

Do not use dishonest standards when measuring length, weight or quantity. Use honest scales and honest weights, an honest ephah and an honest hin. I am the LORD your God, who brought you out of Egypt.

Leviticus 19:35-36

Do not trust in extortion or take pride in stolen goods; though your riches increase, do not set your heart on them.

Psalm 62:10

My son, if sinners entice you, do not give in to them. If they say, "Come along with us; let's lie in wait for someone's blood, let's waylay some harmless soul; let's swallow them alive, like the grave, and whole, like those who go down to the pit; we will get all sorts of valuable things and fill our houses with plunder; throw in your lot with us, and we will share a common purse" — my son, do not go along with them, do not set foot on their paths; for their feet rush into sin, they are swift to shed blood. How useless to spread a net in full view of all the birds! These men lie in wait for their own blood; they waylay only themselves! Such is the end of all who go after ill-gotten gain; it takes away the lives of those who get it.

Proverbs 1:10-19

Men do not despise a thief if he steals to satisfy his hunger when he is starving. Yet if he is caught, he must pay sevenfold, though it costs him all the wealth of his house.

Proverbs 6:30-31

For out of the heart come evil thoughts, murder, adultery, sexual immorality, theft, false testimony, slander.

Matthew 15:19

The commandments, "Do not commit adultery," "Do not murder," "Do not steal," "Do not covet," and whatever other commandment there may be, are summed up in this one rule: "Love your neighbor as yourself."

Romans 13:9

Do you not know that the wicked will not inherit the kingdom of God? Do not be deceived: Neither the sexually immoral nor idolaters nor adulterers nor male prostitutes nor homosexual offenders nor thieves nor the greedy nor drunkards nor slanderers nor swindlers will inherit the kingdom of God.

1 Corinthians 6:9-10

He who has been stealing must steal no longer, but must work, doing something useful with his own hands, that he may have something to share with those in need.

Ephesians 4:28

Avoiding Sexual Temptation @ Work

You shall not commit adultery.

Exodus 20:14

Wisdom will save you from the ways of wicked men, from men whose words are perverse, who leave the straight paths to walk in dark ways, who delight in doing wrong and rejoice in the perverseness of evil, whose paths are crooked and who are devious in their ways. It will save you also from the adulteress, from the wayward wife with her seductive words, who has left the partner of her youth and ignored the covenant she made before God. For her house leads down to death and her paths to the spirits of the dead. None who go to her return or attain the paths of life. Thus you will walk in the ways of good men and keep to the paths of the righteous.

Proverbs 2:12-20

My son, pay attention to my wisdom, listen well to my words of insight, that you may maintain discretion and your lips may preserve knowledge. For the lips of an adulteress drip honey, and her speech is smoother than oil; but in the end she is bitter as gall, sharp as a double-edged sword. Her feet go down to death; her steps lead straight to the grave. She gives no thought to the way of life; her paths are crooked, but she knows it not. Now then, my sons, listen to me; do not turn aside from

237

what I say. Keep to a path far from her, do not go near the door of her house, lest you give your best strength to others and your years to one who is cruel, lest strangers feast on your wealth and your toil enrich another man's house. At the end of your life you will groan, when your flesh and body are spent. You will say, How I hated discipline! How my heart spurned correction! I would not obey my teachers or listen to my instructors. I have come to the brink of utter ruin in the midst of the whole assembly. Drink waters from your own cistern, running water from your own well. Should your springs overflow in the streets, your streams of water in the public squares? Let them be yours alone, never to be shared with strangers. May your fountain be blessed, and my you rejoice in the wife of your youth. A loving doe, a graceful deer — may her breast satisfy you always, may you ever be captivated by her love. Why be captivated, my son, by an adulteress? Why embrace the bosom of another man's wife? For a man's ways are in full view of the LORD, and he examines all his paths. The evil deeds of a wicked man ensnare him; the cords of his sin hold him fast. He will die for lack of discipline, led astray by his own great folly.

Proverbs 5:1-23

For these commands are a lamp, this teaching is a light, and the corrections of discipline are the way to life, keeping you from the immoral woman, from the smooth tongue of the wayward wife. Do not lust in your heart after her beauty or let her captivate you with her eyes, for the prostitute reduces you to a loaf of bread, and the adulteress preys upon your very life. Can a man scoop fire into his lap without his clothes being burned? Can a man walk on hot coals without his feet being scorched? So is he who sleeps with another man's wife; no one who touches her will go unpunished.

Proverbs 6:23-29

But a man who commits adultery lacks judgment; whoever does so destroys himself. Blows and disgrace are his lot, and his shame will never be wiped away; for jealousy arouses a husband's fury, and he will show no mercy when he takes revenge. He will not accept any compensation; he will refuse the bribe, however great it is.

Proverbs 6:32-35

He was going down the street near her corner, walking along in the direction of her house at twilight, as the day was fading, as the dark of night set in. Then out came a woman to meet him, dressed like a prostitute and with crafty intent. (She is loud and defiant, her feet never stay at home; now in the street, now in the squares, at every corner she lurks.) She took hold of him and kissed him and with a brazen face she said: "I have fellowship offerings at home; today I fulfilled my vows. So I came out to meet you; I looked for you and have found you! I have covered my bed with colored linens from Egypt. I have perfumed my bed with myrrh, aloes and cinnamon. Come, let's drink deep of love till morning; let's enjoy ourselves with love! My husband is not at home; he has gone on a long journey. He took his purse filled with money and will not be home till full moon." With persuasive words she led him astray; she seduced him with her smooth talk. All at once he followed her like an ox going to the slaughter, like a deer stepping into a noose till an arrow pierces his liver, like a bird darting into a snare, little knowing it will cost him his life. Now then, my sons, listen to me; pay attention to what I say. Do not let your heart turn to her ways or stray into her paths. Many are the victims she has brought down; her slain are a mighty throng. Her house is a highway to the grave, leading down to the chambers of death.

Proverbs 7:8-27

The woman Folly is loud; she is undisciplined and without knowledge. She sits at the door of her house, on a seat at the highest point of the city, calling out to those who pass by, who go straight on their way. "Let all who are simple come in here!" she says to those who lack judgment. Stolen water is sweet; food eaten in secret is delicious! But little do they know that the dead are there, that her guests are in the depths of the grave.

Proverbs 9:13-18

My son, give me your heart and let your eyes keep to my ways, for a prostitute is a deep pit and a wayward wife is a narrow well. Like a bandit she lies in wait, and multiplies the unfaithful among men.

Proverbs 23:26-28

Like a bird that strays from its nest is a man who strays from his home.

Proverbs 27:8

A man who loves wisdom brings joy to his father, but a companion of prostitutes squanders his wealth.

Proverbs 29:3

Do not spend your strength on women, your vigor on those who ruin kings.

Proverbs 31:3

I find more bitter than death the woman who is a snare, whose heart is a trap and whose hands are chains. The man who pleases God will escape her, but the sinner she will ensnare.

Ecclessiastes 7:26

"You have heard that it was said, 'Do not commit adultery.' But I tell you that anyone who looks at a woman lustfully has already committed adultery with her in his heart."

Matthew 5:27-28

Watch and pray so that you will not fall into temptation. The spirit is willing, but the body is weak.

Matthew 26:41

Therefore do not let sin reign in your mortal body so that you obey its evil desires. Do not offer the parts of your body to sin, as instruments of wickedness, but rather offer yourselves to God, as those who have been brought from death to life; and offer the parts of your body to him as instruments of righteousness.

Romans 6:12-13

Those who live according to the sinful nature have their minds set on what that nature desires; but those who live in accordance with the Spirit have their minds set on what the Spirit desires. The mind of sinful man is death, but the mind controlled by the Spirit is life and peace; the sinful mind is hostile to God. It does not submit to God's law, nor can it do so. Those controlled by the sinful nature cannot please God. You, however, are controlled not by the sinful nature but by the Spirit, if the Spirit of God lives in you.

Romans 8:5-9

Let us behave decently, as in the daytime, not in orgies and drunkenness, not in sexual immorality and debauchery, not in dissension and jealousy. Rather, clothe yourselves with the Lord Jesus Christ, and do not think about how to gratify the desires of the sinful nature.

Romans 13:13-14

I have written you in my letter not to associate with sexually immoral people — not at all meaning the people of this world who are immoral, or the greedy and swindlers, or idolaters. In that case you would have to leave this world. But now I am writing you that you must not associate with anyone who calls himself a brother but is sexually immoral or greedy, an idolater or a slanderer, a drunkard or a swindler. With such a man do not even eat. What business is it of mine to judge those outside the church? Are you not to judge those inside? God will judge those outside. Expel the wicked man from among you.

1 Corinthians 5:9-13

The body is not meant for sexual immorality, but for the Lord, and the Lord for the body. Do you not know that your bodies are members of Christ himself? Shall I then take the members of Christ and unite them with a prostitute? Never! Do you not know that he who unites himself with a prostitute is one with her in body? For it is said, "The two will become one flesh." But he who unites himself with the Lord is one with him in spirit. Flee from sexual immorality. All other sins a man commits are outside his body, but he who sins sexually sins against his own body. Do you not know that your body is a temple of the Holy Spirit, who is in you, whom you have received from God? You are not your own; you were bought at a price. Therefore honor God with your body.

1 Corinthians 6:13, 15-20

But since there is so much immorality, each man should have his own wife, and each woman her own husband. The husband should fulfill his marital duty to his wife, and likewise the wife to her husband. The wife's body does not belong to her alone but also to her husband. In the same way, the husband's body does not belong to him alone but also to his wife. Do not deprive each other except by mutual consent and for a time, so that you may devote yourselves to prayer. Then come together again so that Satan will not tempt you because of your lack of self-control.

1 Corinthians 7:2-5

No temptation has seized you except what is common to man. And God is faithful; he will not let you be tempted beyond what you can bear. But when you are tempted, he will also provide a way out so that you can stand up under it.

1 Corinthians 10:13

So I say, live by the Spirit, and you will not gratify the desires of the sinful nature. For the sinful nature desires what is contrary to the Spirit, and the Spirit what is contrary to the sinful nature. They are in conflict with each other, so that you do not do what you want.

Galatians 5:16-17

The acts of the sinful nature are obvious: sexual immorality, impurity and debauchery; idolatry and witchcraft; hatred, discord, jealousy, fits of rage, selfish ambition, dissensions, factions and envy; drunkenness, orgies, and the like. I warn you, as I did before, that those who live like this will not inherit the kingdom of God. But the fruit of the Spirit is love, joy, peace, patience, kindness, goodness, faithfulness, gentleness and self-control. Against such things there is no law. Those who belong to Christ Jesus have crucified the sinful nature with its passions and desires.

Galatians 5:19-24

Be imitators of God, therefore, as dearly loved children and live a life of love, just as Christ loved us and gave himself up for us as a fragrant offering and sacrifice to God. But among you there must not be even a hint of sexual immorality, or of any kind of impurity, or of greed, be-cause these are improper for God's holy people. Nor should there be obscenity, foolish talk or coarse joking, which are out of place, but rather thanksgiving. For of this you can be sure: No immoral, impure or greedy person — such a man is an idolater — has any inheritance in the kingdom of Christ and of God.

Ephesians 5:1-5

Put on the full armor of God so that you can take your stand against the devil's schemes. For our struggle is not against flesh and blood, but against the rulers, against the authorities, against the powers of this dark world and against the spiritual forces of evil in the heavenly realms. Therefore put on the full armor of God, so that when the day of evil comes, you may be able to stand your ground, and after you have done everything, to stand. Stand firm then, with the belt of truth buckled around your waist, with the breastplate of righteousness in place, and with your feet fitted with the readiness that comes from the gospel of peace. In addition to all this, take up the shield of faith, with which you can extinguish all the flaming arrows of the evil one. Take the helmet of salvation and the sword of the Spirit, which is the word of God. And pray in the Spirit on all occasions with all kinds of prayers and requests. With this in mind, be alert and always keep on praying for all the saints.

Ephesians 6:11-18

Finally, brothers, we instructed you how to live in order to please God, as in fact you are living. Now we ask you and urge you in the Lord Jesus to do this more and more. For you know what instructions we gave you by the authority of the Lord Jesus. It is God's will that you should be sanctified: that you should avoid sexual immorality; that each of you should learn to control his own body in a way that is holy and honorable, not in passionate lust like the heathen, who do not know God; and that in this matter no one should wrong his brother or take advantage of him. The Lord will punish men for all such sins, as we have already told you and warned you. For God did not call us to be impure, but to live a holy life.

1 Thessalonians 4:1-7

Marriage should be honored by all, and the marriage bed kept pure, for God will judge the adulterer and all the sexually immoral.

Hebrews 13:4

When tempted, no one should say, "God is tempting me." For God cannot be tempted by evil, nor does he tempt anyone; but each one is tempted when, by his own evil desire, he is dragged away and enticed. Then, after desire has conceived, it gives birth to sin; and sin, when it is full-grown, gives birth to death.

James 1:13-15

Submit yourselves, then, to God. Resist the devil, and he will flee from you. Come near to God and he will come near to you

James 4:7-8

For everything in the world — the cravings of sinful man, the lust of his eyes and the boasting of what he has and does — comes not from the Father but from the world. The world and its desires pass away, but the man who does the will of God lives forever.

1 John 2:16-17

You, dear children, are from God and have overcome them, because the one who is in you is greater than the one who is in the world.

1 John 4:4

Part Four

Interaction

@ Work

People Skills
@ Work

A gentle answer turns away wrath, but a harsh word stirs up anger.

Proverbs 15:1

Starting a quarrel is like breaching a dam; so drop the matter before a dispute breaks out.

Proverbs 17:14

A man's wisdom gives him patience; it is to his glory to overlook an offense.

Proverbs 19:11

Blessed are the peacemakers, for they will be called sons of God.

Matthew 5:9

So watch yourselves. "If your brother sins, rebuke him, and if he repents, forgive him. If he sins against you seven times in a day, and seven times comes back to you and says, 'I repent,' forgive him."

Luke 17:3-4

Be devoted to one another in brotherly love. Honor one another above yourselves. Bless those who persecute you; bless and do not curse. Live in harmony with one another. Do not be proud, but be willing to associate with people of low position. Do not be conceited. Do not repay anyone evil for evil. Be careful to do what is right in the eyes of everybody. If it is possible, as far as it depends on you, live at peace with everyone. Do not take revenge, my friends, but leave room for God's wrath, for it is written: "It is mine to avenge; I will repay," says the Lord. On the contrary: "If your enemy is hungry, feed him; if he is thirsty, give him something to drink. In doing this, you will heap burning coals on his head." Do not be overcome by evil, but overcome evil with good.

Romans 12:10,14,16-21

So then, each of us will give an account of himself to God. Therefore let us stop passing judgment on one another. Instead, make up your mind not to put any stumbling block or obstacle in your brother's way. Let us therefore make every effort to do what leads to peace and to mutual edification.

Romans 14:12-13,19

Accept one another, then, just as Christ accepted you, in order to bring praise to God.

Romans 15:7

Make every effort to keep the unity of the Spirit through the bond of peace. Therefore each of you must put off falsehood and speak truthfully to his neighbor, for we are all members of one body. In your anger do not sin: Do not let the sun go down while you are still angry, and do not give the devil a foothold. Do not let any unwholesome talk come out of your mouths, but only what is helpful for building others up according to their needs, that it may benefit those who listen. Get rid of all bitterness, rage and anger, brawling and slander, along with every form of malice. Be kind and compassionate to one another, forgiving each other, just as in Christ God forgave you.

Ephesians 4:3,25-27,29,31-32

Submit to one another out of reverence for Christ.

Ephesians 5:21

Do nothing out of selfish ambition or vain conceit, but in humility consider others better than yourselves. Each of you should look not only to your own interests, but also to the interests of others. Do everything without complaining or arguing.

Philippians 2:3-4,14

Do not lie to each other, since you have taken off your old self with its practices Therefore, as God's chosen people, holy and dearly loved, clothe yourselves with compassion, kindness, humility, gentleness and patience. Bear with each other and forgive whatever grievances you may have against one another. Forgive as the Lord forgave you. And over all these virtues put on love, which binds them all together in perfect unity.

Colossians 3:9,12-14

Make sure that nobody pays back wrong for wrong, but always try to be kind to each other and to everyone else.

1 Thessalonians 5:15

Don't have anything to do with foolish and stupid arguments, because you know they produce quarrels. And the Lord's servant must not quarrel; instead, he must be kind to everyone, able to teach, not resentful. Those who oppose him he must gently instruct, in the hope that God will grant them repentance leading them to a knowledge of the truth, and that they will come to their senses and escape from the trap of the devil, who has taken them captive to do his will.

2 Timothy 2:23-26

And let us consider how we may spur one another on toward love and good deeds.

Hebrews 10:24

Make every effort to live in peace with all men and to be holy; without holiness no one will see the Lord.

Hebrews 12:14

My dear brothers, take note of this: Everyone should be quick to listen, slow to speak and slow to become angry, for man's anger does not bring about the righteous life that God desires.

James 1:19-20

Each one should use whatever gift he has received to serve others, faithfully administering God's grace in its various forms. If anyone speaks, he should do it as one speaking the very words of God. If anyone serves, he should do it with the strength God provides, so that in all things God may be praised through Jesus Christ. To him be the glory and the power for ever and ever. Amen.

1 Peter 4:10-11

Choosing the Correct Relationships @ Work

Interaction @ Work

Blessed is the man who does not walk in the counsel of the wicked or stand in the way of sinners or sit in the seat of mockers. But his delight is in the law of the LORD, and on his law he meditates day and night. He is like a tree planted by streams of water, which yields its fruit in season and whose leaf does not wither. Whatever he does prospers.

Psalm 1:1-3

Vindicate me, O LORD, for I have led a blameless life; I have trusted in the LORD without wavering. Test me, O LORD, and try me, examine my heart and my mind; for your love is ever before me, and I walk continually in your truth. I do not sit with deceitful men, nor do I consort with hypocrites; I abhor the assembly of evildoers and refuse to sit with the wicked. I wash my hands in innocence, and go about your altar, O LORD, proclaiming aloud your praise and telling of all your wonderful deeds. I love the house where you live, O LORD, the place where your glory dwells. Do not take away my soul along with sinners, my life with bloodthirsty men, in whose hands are wicked schemes, whose right hands are full of bribes. But I lead a blameless life; redeem me and be merciful to me. My feet stand on level ground; in the great assembly I will praise the LORD.

Psalm 26:1-12

I will sing of your love and justice; to you, O LORD, I will sing praise. I will be careful to lead a blameless life — when will you come to me? I will walk in my house with blameless heart. I will set before my eyes no vile thing. The deeds of faithless men I hate; they will not cling to me. Men of perverse heart shall be far from me; I will have nothing to do with evil. Whoever slanders his neighbor in secret, him will I put to silence; whoever has haughty eyes and a proud heart, him will I not endure. My eyes will be on the faithful in the land, that they may dwell with me; he whose walk is blameless will minister to me. No one who practices deceit will dwell in my house; no one who speaks falsely will stand in my presence. Every morning I will put to silence all the wicked in the land; I will cut off every evildoer from the city of the LORD.

Psalm 101:1-8

I am a friend to all who fear you, to all who follow your precepts. The earth is filled with your love, O LORD; teach me your decrees.

Psalm 119:63-64

Away from me, you evildoers, that I may keep the commands of my God!

Psalm 119:115

Let not my heart be drawn to what is evil, to take part in wicked deeds with men who are evildoers; let me not eat of their delicacies.

Psalm 141:4

My son, if sinners entice you, do not give in to them. If they say, "Come along with us; let's lie in wait for someone's blood, let's waylay some harmless soul; let's swallow them alive, like the grave, and whole, like those who go down to the pit; we will get all sorts of valuable things and fill our houses with plunder; throw in your lot with us, and we will share a common purse" — my son, do not go along with them, do not set foot on their paths; for their feet rush into sin, they are swift to shed blood. How useless to spread a net in full view of all the birds! These men lie in wait for their own blood; they waylay only themselves! Such is the end of all who go after ill-gotten gain; it takes away the lives of those who get it.

Proverbs 1:10-19

Wisdom will save you from the ways of wicked men, from men whose words are perverse, who leave the straight paths to walk in dark ways, who delight in doing wrong and rejoice in the perverseness of evil, whose paths are crooked and who are devious in their ways. It will save you also from the adulteress, from the wayward wife with her seductive words, who has left the partner of her youth and ignored the covenant she made before God. For her house leads down to death and her paths to the spirits of the dead. None who go to her return or attain the paths of life. Thus you will walk in the ways of good men and keep to the paths of the righteous. For the upright will live in the land, and the blameless will remain in it; but the wicked will be cut off from the land, and the unfaithful will be torn from it.

Proverbs 2:12-22

Do not set foot on the path of the wicked or walk in the way of evil men. Avoid it, do not travel on it; turn from it and go on your way. For they cannot sleep till they do evil; they are robbed of slumber till they make someone fall. They eat the bread of wickedness and drink the wine of violence.

Proverbs 4:14-17

A righteous man is cautious in friendship, but the way of the wicked leads them astray.

Proverbs 12:26

He who walks with the wise grows wise, but a companion of fools suffers harm.

Proverbs 13:20

Stay away from a foolish man, for you will not find knowledge on his lips.

Proverbs 14:7

A friend loves at all times, and a brother is born for adversity.

Proverbs 17:17

A man of many companions may come to ruin, but there is a friend who sticks closer than a brother.

Proverbs 18:24

Wealth brings many friends, but a poor man's friend deserts him.
Proverbs 19:4

A poor man is shunned by all his relatives — how much more do his friends avoid him! Though he pursues them with pleading, they are nowhere to be found.
Proverbs 19:7

He who loves a pure heart and whose speech is gracious will have the king for his friend.
Proverbs 22:11

Do not make friends with a hot-tempered man, do not associate with one easily angered, or you may learn his ways and get yourself ensnared.
Proverbs 22:24-25

Do not join those who drink too much wine or gorge themselves on meat, for drunkards and gluttons become poor, and drowsiness clothes them in rags.
Proverbs 23:20-21

Do not envy wicked men, do not desire their company; for their hearts plot violence, and their lips talk about making trouble.
Proverbs 24:1-2

Do not fret because of evil men or be envious of the wicked, for the evil man has no future hope, and the lamp of the wicked will be snuffed out. Fear the LORD and the king, my son, and do not join with the rebellious,
Proverbs 24:19-21

Wounds from a friend can be trusted, but an enemy multiplies kisses.
Proverbs 27:6

Perfume and incense bring joy to the heart, and the pleasantness of one's friend springs from his earnest counsel.
Proverbs 27:9

Do not forsake your friend and the friend of your father, and do not go to your brother's house when disaster strikes you — better a neighbor nearby than a brother far away.
Proverbs 27:10

As iron sharpens iron, so one man sharpens another.

Proverbs 27:17

He who keeps the law is a discerning son, but a companion of gluttons disgraces his father.

Proverbs 28:7

A man who loves wisdom brings joy to his father, but a companion of prostitutes squanders his wealth.

Proverbs 29:3

But now I am writing you that you must not associate with anyone who calls himself a brother but is sexually immoral or greedy, an idolater or a slanderer, a drunkard or a swindler. With such a man do not even eat.

1 Corinthians 5:11

Do not be misled: Bad company corrupts good character.

1 Corinthians 15:33

Do not be yoked together with unbelievers. For what do righteousness and wickedness have in common? Or what fellowship can light have with darkness? What harmony is there between Christ and Belial? What does a believer have in common with an unbeliever? What agreement is there between the temple of God and idols? For we are the temple of the living God. As God has said: "I will live with them and walk among them, and I will be their God, and they will be my people. Therefore, come out from them and be separate," says the Lord. "Touch no unclean thing, and I will receive you. I will be a Father to you, and you will be my sons and daughters," says the Lord Almighty.

2 Corinthians 6:14-18

Be imitators of God, therefore, as dearly loved children and live a life of love, just as Christ loved us and gave himself up for us as a fragrant offering and sacrifice to God. But among you there must not be even a hint of sexual immorality, or of any kind of impurity, or of greed, because these are improper for God's holy people. Nor should there be obscenity, foolish talk or coarse joking, which are out of place, but rather thanksgiving. For of this you can be sure: No immoral, impure or greedy person — such a man is an idolater — has any inheritance in the kingdom of Christ and of God. Let no one deceive you with empty words, for because of such things God's wrath comes on those who are disobedient. Therefore do not be partners with them. For you were once darkness, but now you are light in the Lord. Live as children of light (for the fruit of the light consists in all goodness, righteousness and truth) and find out what pleases the Lord. Have nothing to do with the fruitless deeds of darkness, but rather expose them.

Ephesians 5:1-11

Avoid godless chatter, because those who indulge in it will become more and more ungodly.

2 Timothy 2:16

And let us consider how we may spur one another on toward love and good deeds. Let us not give up meeting together, as some are in the habit of doing, but let us encourage one another — and all the more as you see the Day approaching.

Hebrews 10:24-25

You adulterous people, don't you know that friendship with the world is hatred toward God? Anyone who chooses to be a friend of the world becomes an enemy of God.

James 4:4

Choosing the Correct Advisors @ Work

But select capable men from all the people — men who fear God, trustworthy men who hate dishonest gain — and appoint them as officials over thousands, hundreds, fifties and tens.

Exodus 18:21

Blessed is the man who does not walk in the counsel of the wicked or stand in the way of sinners or sit in the seat of mockers. But his delight is in the law of the LORD, and on his law he meditates day and night. He is like a tree planted by streams of water, which yields its fruit in season and whose leaf does not wither. Whatever he does prospers.

Psalm 1:1-3

Vindicate me, O LORD, for I have led a blameless life; I have trusted in the LORD without wavering. Test me, O LORD, and try me, examine my heart and my mind; for your love is ever before me, and I walk continually in your truth. I do not sit with deceitful men, nor do I consort with hypocrites; I abhor the assembly of evildoers and refuse to sit with the wicked. I wash my hands in innocence, and go about your altar, O LORD, proclaiming aloud your praise and telling of all your wonderful deeds. I love the house where you live, O LORD, the place where your glory dwells. Do not take away my soul along with sinners, my life with blood-thirsty men, in whose hands are wicked schemes, whose right hands are full of bribes. But I lead a blameless life; redeem me and be merciful to me. My feet stand on level ground; in the great assembly I will praise the LORD.

Psalm 26:1-12

I will sing of your love and justice; to you, O LORD, I will sing praise. I will be careful to lead a blameless life — when will you come to me? I will walk in my house with blameless heart. I will set before my eyes no vile thing. The deeds of faithless men I hate; they will not cling to me. Men of perverse heart shall be far from me; I will have nothing to do with evil. Whoever slanders his neighbor in secret, him will I put to silence; whoever has haughty eyes and a proud heart, him will I not endure. My eyes will be on the faithful in the land, that they may dwell with me; he whose walk is blameless will minister to me. No one who practices deceit will dwell in my house; no one who speaks falsely will stand in my presence. Every morning I will put to silence all the wicked in the land; I will cut off every evildoer from the city of the LORD.

Psalm 101:1-8

Instruct a wise man and he will be wiser still; teach a righteous man and he will add to his learning.

Proverbs 9:9

The man of integrity walks securely, but he who takes crooked paths will be found out.

Proverbs 10:9

The integrity of the upright guides them, but the unfaithful are destroyed by their duplicity.

Proverbs 11:3

For lack of guidance a nation falls, but many advisers make victory sure.

Proverbs 11:14

The plans of the righteous are just, but the advice of the wicked is deceitful.

Proverbs 12:5

The way of a fool seems right to him, but a wise man listens to advice.
Proverbs 12:15

A righteous man is cautious in friendship, but the way of the wicked leads them astray.
Proverbs 12:26

Pride only breeds quarrels, but wisdom is found in those who take advice.
Proverbs 13:10

The teaching of the wise is a fountain of life, turning a man from the snares of death.
Proverbs 13:14

He who ignores discipline comes to poverty and shame, but whoever heeds correction is honored.
Proverbs 13:18

He who walks with the wise grows wise, but a companion of fools suffers harm.
Proverbs 13:20

Stay away from a foolish man, for you will not find knowledge on his lips.
Proverbs 14:7

A mocker resents correction; he will not consult the wise.
Proverbs 15:12

Plans fail for lack of counsel, but with many advisers they succeed.
Proverbs 15:22

He who listens to a life-giving rebuke will be at home among the wise. He who ignores discipline despises himself, but whoever heeds correction gains understanding.
Proverbs 15:31-32

The heart of the discerning acquires knowledge; the ears of the wise seek it out.
Proverbs 18:15

Listen to advice and accept instruction, and in the end you will be wise.

Proverbs 19:20

Make plans by seeking advice; if you wage war, obtain guidance.

Proverbs 20:18

When a mocker is punished, the simple gain wisdom; when a wise man is instructed, he gets knowledge.

Proverbs 21:11

For waging war you need guidance, and for victory many advisers.

Proverbs 24:6

As iron sharpens iron, so one man sharpens another.

Proverbs 27:17

Do not be misled: Bad company corrupts good character.

1 Corinthians 15:33

Watching What You Say @ Work

Do not accuse a man for no reason — when he has done you no harm.

Proverbs 3:30

The wise in heart accept commands, but a chattering fool comes to ruin.

Proverbs 10:8

He who winks maliciously causes grief, and a chattering fool comes to ruin.

Proverbs 10:10

Wise men store up knowledge, but the mouth of a fool invites ruin.

Proverbs 10:14

With his mouth the godless destroys his neighbor, but through knowledge the righteous escape.

Proverbs 11:9

Through the blessing of the upright a city is exalted, but by the mouth of the wicked it is destroyed.

Proverbs 11:11

An evil man is trapped by his sinful talk, but a righteous man escapes trouble. From the fruit of his lips a man is filled with good things as surely as the work of his hands rewards him.

Proverbs 12:13-14

An anxious heart weighs a man down, but a kind word cheers him up.

Proverbs 12:25

A fool's talk brings a rod to his back, but the lips of the wise protect them.

Proverbs 14:3

The lips of the wise spread knowledge; not so the hearts of fools.

Proverbs 15:7

A cheerful look brings joy to the heart, and good news gives health to the bones.

Proverbs 15:30

A scoundrel plots evil, and his speech is like a scorching fire.

Proverbs 16:27

He who covers over an offense promotes love, but whoever repeats the matter separates close friends.

Proverbs 17:9

A man of perverse heart does not prosper; he whose tongue is deceitful falls into trouble.

Proverbs 17:20

A fool finds no pleasure in understanding but delights in airing his own opinions.

Proverbs 18:2

He who answers before listening — that is his folly and his shame.

Proverbs 18:13

An offended brother is more unyielding than a fortified city, and disputes are like the barred gates of a citadel.

Proverbs 18:19

From the fruit of his mouth a man's stomach is filled; with the harvest from his lips he is satisfied. The tongue has the power of life and death, and those who love it will eat its fruit.

Proverbs 18:20-21

A false witness will not go unpunished, and he who pours out lies will not go free.

Proverbs 19:5

A false witness will not go unpunished, and he who pours out lies will perish.

Proverbs 19:9

A gossip betrays a confidence; so avoid a man who talks too much.

Proverbs 20:19

It is a trap for a man to dedicate something rashly and only later to consider his vows.

Proverbs 20:25

My son, if your heart is wise, then my heart will be glad; my inmost being will rejoice when your lips speak what is right.

Proverbs 23:15-16

Do not testify against your neighbor without cause, or use your lips to deceive.

Proverbs 24:28

Like a fluttering sparrow or a darting swallow, an undeserved curse does not come to rest.

Proverbs 26:2

Do not answer a fool according to his folly, or you will be like him yourself.

Proverbs 26:4

Like a coating of glaze over earthenware are fervent lips with an evil heart.

Proverbs 26:23

If a man loudly blesses his neighbor early in the morning, it will be taken as a curse.

Proverbs 27:14

Whoever flatters his neighbor is spreading a net for his feet.

Proverbs 29:5

Gossip and Slander @ Work

Do not spread false reports. Do not help a wicked man by being a malicious witness. Do not follow the crowd in doing wrong. When you give testimony in a lawsuit, do not pervert justice by siding with the crowd.

Exodus 23:1-2

Do not go about spreading slander among your people. Do not do anything that endangers your neighbor's life. I am the LORD.

Leviticus 19:16

LORD, who may dwell in your sanctuary? Who may live on your holy hill? He whose walk is blameless and who does what is righteous, who speaks the truth from his heart and has no slander on his tongue, who does his neighbor no wrong and casts no slur on his fellowman, who despises a vile man but honors those who fear the LORD, who keeps his oath even when it hurts, who lends his money without usury and does not accept a bribe against the innocent. He who does these things will never be shaken.

Psalm 15:1-5

Whoever of you loves life and desires to see many good days, keep your tongue from evil and your lips from speaking lies. Turn from evil and do good; seek peace and pursue it.

Psalm 34:12-14

Whoever slanders his neighbor in secret, him will I put to silence; whoever has haughty eyes and a proud heart, him will I not endure.

Psalm 101:5

Let slanderers not be established in the land; may disaster hunt down men of violence.

Psalm 140:11

Put away perversity from your mouth; keep corrupt talk far from your lips.

Proverbs 4:24

There are six things the LORD hates, seven that are detestable to him: haughty eyes, a lying tongue, hands that shed innocent blood, a heart that devises wicked schemes, feet that are quick to rush into evil, a false witness who pours out lies and a man who stirs up dissension among brothers.

Proverbs 6:16-19

To fear the LORD is to hate evil; I hate pride and arrogance, evil behavior and perverse speech.

Proverbs 8:13

He who conceals his hatred has lying lips, and whoever spreads slander is a fool.

Proverbs 10:18

The mouth of the righteous brings forth wisdom, but a perverse tongue will be cut out.

Proverbs 10:31

The lips of the righteous know what is fitting, but the mouth of the wicked only what is perverse.

Proverbs 10:32

With his mouth the godless destroys his neighbor, but through knowledge the righteous escape.

Proverbs 11:9

A gossip betrays a confidence, but a trustworthy man keeps a secret.

Proverbs 11:13

An evil man is trapped by his sinful talk, but a righteous man escapes trouble.

Proverbs 12:13

A truthful witness gives honest testimony, but a false witness tells lies.

Proverbs 12:17

Reckless words pierce like a sword, but the tongue of the wise brings healing.

Proverbs 12:18

Truthful lips endure forever, but a lying tongue lasts only a moment.

Proverbs 12:19

He who guards his lips guards his life, but he who speaks rashly will come to ruin.

Proverbs 13:3

A truthful witness saves lives, but a false witness is deceitful.

Proverbs 14:25

A gentle answer turns away wrath, but a harsh word stirs up anger.

Proverbs 15:1

The tongue of the wise commends knowledge, but the mouth of the fool gushes folly.

Proverbs 15:2

The tongue that brings healing is a tree of life, but a deceitful tongue crushes the spirit.

Proverbs 15:4

A perverse man stirs up dissension, and a gossip separates close friends.

Proverbs 16:28

A wicked man listens to evil lips; a liar pays attention to a malicious tongue.

Proverbs 17:4

He who covers over an offense promotes love, but whoever repeats the matter separates close friends.

Proverbs 17:9

The words of a gossip are like choice morsels; they go down to a man's inmost parts.

Proverbs 18:8

A false witness will not go unpunished, and who pours out lies will not go free.

Proverbs 19:5

A gossip betrays a confidence; so avoid a man who talks too much.

Proverbs 20:19

He who guards his mouth and his tongue keeps himself from calamity.

Proverbs 21:23

Like a fluttering sparrow or a darting swallow, an undeserved curse does come to rest.

Proverbs 26:2

Without wood a fire goes out; without gossip a quarrel dies down.

Proverbs 26:20

The words of a gossip are like choice morsels; they go down to a man's inmost parts.

Proverbs 26:22

Like a coating of glaze over earthenware are fervent lips with an evil heart.

Proverbs 26:23

A lying tongue hates those it hurts, and a flattering mouth works ruin.

Proverbs 26:28

Do not pay attention to every word people say, or you may hear your servant cursing you — for you know in your heart that many times you yourself have cursed others.

Ecclesiastes 7:21-22

Do not revile the king even in your thoughts, or curse the rich in your bedroom, because a bird of the air may carry your words, and a bird on the wing may report what you say.

Ecclesiastes 10:20

Blessed are you when people insult you, persecute you and falsely say all kinds of evil against you because of me. Rejoice and be glad, because great is your reward in heaven, for in the same way they persecuted the prophets who were before you. You are the salt of the earth. But if the salt loses its saltiness, how can it be made salty again? It is no longer good for anything, except to be thrown out and trampled by men. You are the light of the world. A city on a hill cannot be hidden.

Matthew 5:11-14

But I tell you that men will have to give account on the day of judgment for every careless word they have spoken. For by your words you will be acquitted, and by your words you will be condemned.

Matthew 12:36-37

We work hard with our own hands. When we are cursed, we bless; when we are persecuted, we endure it; when we are slandered, we answer kindly.

1 Corinthians 4:12-13

Do you not know that the wicked will not inherit the kingdom of God? Do not be deceived: Neither the sexually immoral nor idolaters nor adulterers nor male prostitutes nor homosexual offenders nor thieves nor the greedy nor drunkards nor slanderers nor swindlers will inherit the kingdom of God. And that is what some of you were. But you were washed, you were sanctified, you were justified in the name of the Lord Jesus Christ and by the Spirit of our God.

1 Corinthians 6:9-11

Therefore each of you must put off falsehood and speak truthfully to his neighbor, for we are all members of one body.

Ephesians 4:25

Do not let any unwholesome talk come out of your mouths, but only what is helpful for building others up according to their needs, that it may benefit those who listen. And do not grieve the Holy Spirit of God, with whom you were sealed for the day of redemption. Get rid of all bitterness, rage and anger, brawling and slander, along with every form of malice. Be kind and compassionate to one another, forgiving each other, just as in Christ God forgave you.

Ephesians 4:29-32

But among you there must not be even a hint of sexual immorality, or of any kind of impurity, or of greed, because these are improper for God's holy people. Nor should there be obscenity, foolish talk or coarse joking, which are out of place, but rather thanksgiving.

Ephesians 5:3-4

In the same way, their wives are to be women worthy of respect, not malicious talkers but temperate and trustworthy in everything.

1 Timothy 3:11

Besides, they get into the habit of being idle and going about from house to house. And not only do they become idlers, but also gossips and busybodies, saying things they ought not to.

1 Timothy 5:13

Likewise, teach the older women to be reverent in the way they live, not to be slanderers or addicted to much wine, but to teach what is good.

Titus 2:3

Remind the people to be subject to rulers and authorities, to be obedient, to be ready to do whatever is good, to slander no one, to be peaceable and considerate, and to show true humility toward all men.

Titus 3:1-2

My dear brothers, take note of this: Everyone should be quick to listen, slow to speak and slow to become angry, for man's anger does not bring about the righteous life that God desires. If anyone considers himself religious and yet does not keep a tight rein on his tongue, he deceives himself and his religion is worthless.

James 1:19-20,26

Likewise the tongue is a small part of the body, but it makes great boasts. Consider what a great forest is set on fire by a small spark. The tongue also is a fire, a world of evil among the parts of the body. It corrupts the whole person, sets the whole course of his life on fire, and is itself set on fire by hell. All kinds of animals, birds, reptiles and creatures of the sea are being tamed and have been tamed by man, but no man can tame the tongue. It is a restless evil, full of deadly poison. With the tongue we praise our Lord and Father, and with it we curse men, who have been made in God's likeness. Out of the same mouth come praise and cursing. My brothers, this should not be.

James 3:5-10

Brothers, do not slander one another. Anyone who speaks against his brother or judges him speaks against the law and judges it. When you judge the law, you are not keeping it, but sitting in judgment on it. There is only one Lawgiver and Judge, the one who is able to save and destroy. But you — who are you to judge your neighbor?

James 4:11-12

Therefore, rid yourselves of all malice and all deceit, hypocrisy, envy, and slander of every kind.

1 Peter 2:1

Do not repay evil with evil or insult with insult, but with blessing, because to this you were called so that you may inherit a blessing. For, Whoever would love life and see good days must keep his tongue from evil and his lips from deceitful speech. But in your hearts set apart Christ as Lord. Always be prepared to give an answer to everyone who asks you to give the reason for the hope that you have. But do this with gentleness and respect, keeping a clear conscience, so that those who speak maliciously against your good behavior in Christ may be ashamed of their slander.

1 Peter 3:9-10,15-16

About the Authors

Dr. J. Victor and Mrs. Catherine B. Eagan are both ordained ministers committed to teaching biblical principles to the body of Christ in the areas of business and finance. Through Word of Faith International Christian Center – Kingdom Business Association (KBA) they serve as Directors of the KBA under the leadership of Bishop Keith A. Butler. They developed, published the curriculum and teach a three-year course of study through The Workplace Wisdom Institute.

The Workplace Wisdom Institute was founded to provide biblical solutions to challenges in the workplace by addressing contemporary issues facing working people. Workplace Wisdom directs people at all levels to practical applications of the Bible in their every day decision-making process.

Dr. J. Victor Eagan is a very successful entrepreneur and has been practicing in the field of dentistry for the past 20 years. Specializing as an orthodontist, he has operated his practice in line with the Word of God. Dr. Eagan completed his undergraduate work at The University of Michigan and received his professional degree from its School of Dentistry. His orthodontic specialty was completed at Howard University, with honors.

Mrs. Catherine B. Eagan has an extensive 25-year financial background. She began her career in banking as a commercial lender and also worked in the area of commercial real estate development. Her diversified experience has allowed her to lend or manage a cumulative portfolio of over $150,000,000. Her most current position prior to becoming an entrepreneur was as a Private Banker. For five years she served as a Vice President and Private Banking Officer for one of Michigan's largest banks. She was a relationship manager for the bank's wealthiest customers and had responsibility for lending, investments, and personal and corporate trust services. She presently manages five of the Eagan Enterprise, Ltd. holdings.

Mrs. Eagan received a Bachelor of Arts degree from Simmons College, Boston, Massachusetts. She was awarded an Ed. M. degree from Harvard University, Cambridge, Massachusetts.

Dr. and Mrs. Eagan are prolific writers and have authored several books; **Taking The Wisdom of God Into the Workplace, Dominating Money Tapping Into God's Supernatural Economy, Using the Power of God to Succeed at Work, Finding and Fulfilling Your Purpose at Work,** and **The Word at Work, Volumes I and II.** Upcoming books include: **Godly Leadership at Work, Godly Character at Work, Workplace Wisdom® Institute Instructor Training Multi-Media Resource Library, The Road to the Wealthy Place, Dominating Money in Business, Eliminating Debt, Budgeting, 10 Keys to Dominating Money,** and **Terminating Conflict Permanently at Work.**

They both love God and passionately seek to continue to grow deeply in the character of Christ. They are international speakers in demand and travel worldwide.

Books and Resources from Workplace Wisdom® Publishing

Taking the Wisdom of God into the Workplace

Using the Power of God to Succeed at Work
Operating at the Top of the Game

Finding and Fulfilling Your Purpose at Work
Mastering Performance

Dominating Money
Tapping Into God's Supernatural Economy

The Word @ Work, Scriptures for the Workplace — Volume Two

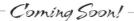

Coming Soon!

Godly Leadership at Work

Godly Character at Work

Workplace Wisdom® Institute Instructor Training
Multi-Media Resource Library

10 Keys to Dominating Money

Eliminating Debt

Budgeting

The Road to the Wealthy Place
Dominating Money in Business

Terminating Conflict Permanently at Work